Access to History

General Editor: Keith Randell

Elizabeth I and the
Government of England

Access to History

General Editor: Keith Randell

Elizabeth I and the Government of England

Keith Randell

A MEMBER OF THE HODDER HEADLINE GROUP

The cover illustration shows a portrait of Elizabeth I, attributed to Robert Peake the Elder (Private Collection).

To Molly Parsons, with love and thanks for 30 years of unfailing support.

Order: Please contact Bookpoint Ltd, 130 Milton Park, Abingdon, Oxon OX14 4SB. Telephone: (44) 01235 827720. Fax: (44) 01235 400454. Lines are open from 9.00-6.00, Monday to Saturday, with a 24-hour message answering service. You can also order through our website www.hoddereducation.co.uk

British Library Cataloguing in Publication Data
A catalogue record for this title is available from The British Library

ISBN-10: 0–340–56547–0
ISBN-13: 978 0–340–56547–6

First published 1994
Impression number   12   11   10   9
Year   2010   2009   2008   2007   2006   2005

Typeset by Sempringham Publishing, Bedford.
Printed in Great Britain for Hodder Murray, an imprint of Hodder Education, a member of the Hodder Headline Group, 338, Euston Road, London NW1 3BH by CPI Bath

Contents

Contents

Preface

To the general reader

Although the *Access to History* series has been designed with the needs of students studying the subject at higher examination levels very much in mind, it also has a great deal to offer the general reader. The main body of the text (i.e. ignoring the Study Guides at the ends of chapters) forms a readable and yet stimulating survey of a coherent topic as studied by historians. However, each author's aim has not merely been to provide a clear explanation of what happened in the past (to interest and inform): it has also been assumed that most readers wish to be stimulated into thinking further about the topic and to form opinions of their own about the significance of the events that are described and discussed (to be challenged). Thus, although no prior knowledge of the topic is expected on the reader's part, she or he is treated as an intelligent and thinking person throughout. The author tends to share ideas and possibilities with the reader, rather than passing on numbers of so-called 'historical truths'.

To the student reader

There are many ways in which the series can be used by students studying History at a higher level. It will, therefore, be worthwhile thinking about your own study strategy before you start your work on this book. Obviously, your strategy will vary depending on the aim you have in mind, and the time for study that is available to you.

If, for example, you want to acquire a general overview of the topic in the shortest possible time, the following approach will probably be the most effective:

1 Read chapter 1 and think about its contents.
2 Read the 'Making notes' section at the end of chapter 2 and decide whether it is necessary for you to read this chapter.
3 If it is, read the chapter, stopping at each heading to note down the main points that have been made.
4 Repeat stage 2 (and stage 3 where appropriate) for all the other chapters.

If, however, your aim is to gain a thorough grasp of the topic, taking however much time is necessary to do so, you may benefit from carrying out the same procedure with each chapter, as follows:

1 Read the chapter as fast as you can, and preferably at one sitting.
2 Study the flow diagram at the end of the chapter, ensuring that you understand the general 'shape' of what you have just read.

3 Read the 'Making notes' section (and the 'Answering essay questions' section, if there is one) and decide what further work you need to do on the chapter. In particularly important sections of the book, this will involve reading the chapter a second time and stopping at each heading to think about (and to write a summary of) what you have just read.

4 Attempt the 'Source-based questions' section. It will sometimes be sufficient to think through your answers, but additional understanding will often be gained by forcing yourself to write them down.

When you have finished the main chapters of the book, study the 'Further Reading' section and decide what additional reading (if any) you will do on the topic.

This book has been designed to help make your studies both enjoyable and successful. If you can think of ways in which this could have been done more effectively, please write to tell me. In the meantime, I hope that you will gain greatly from your study of History.

Keith Randell

Acknowledgements

The Publishers would like to thank the following for permission to reproduce illustrations in this volume:

Cover - Elizabeth I attributed to Robert Peake the Elder, Private Collection. Bodleian Library, Oxford p. 54; National Portrait Gallery, London p. 67 and p. 125.

Every effort has been made to trace and acknowledge ownership of copyright. The Publishers will be glad to make suitable arrangements with any copyright holders whom it has not been possible to contact.

CHAPTER 1

Introduction

If most people were asked to name the woman who has had the greatest impact on British political history they would probably name Margaret Thatcher. A generation ago the choice would almost certainly have been Queen Elizabeth I, as it would also have been for the whole of the time since the emergence of History as an academic discipline in the mid-nineteenth century. In fact, Elizabeth would have been on any short list of outstanding British political figures, irrespective of gender. Especially during the century when the British considered themselves to be a superior race (c1850-c1950) she was popularly thought of as typifying this greatness. She was portrayed as the majestic Virgin Queen, the caring mother figure of her adoring people, presiding over an era of national triumph, when enemies were scattered (the defeat of the Spanish Armada), fearless seamen (Sir Francis Drake, Sir Walter Ralegh etc) performed deeds of daring in their mistress's name, and artistic achievement reached hitherto unimagined heights (William Shakespeare, Christopher Marlowe etc). It was as if the sun had shone on a chosen island people whose confidence was limitless and who were taking their cue from their beloved Sovereign Lady. Sentimental, and largely uncritical, accounts of her life (1533-1603) and of her reign (1558-1603) were produced in abundance and generations of school children were taught to be especially proud of this glorious portion of their national heritage.

In particular, Elizabethan England was portrayed as a vibrant society which for the first time was becoming aware of a national destiny that over several centuries was to transform the southern half of a remote island on Europe's periphery into the possessor of the most extensive empire the world had ever known. Much was made of the birth of an English nationalism that was said to have been fashioned from the successful struggle of a newly Protestant state against the might of Catholic Europe, personified by Philip II of Spain, and that was typified by the heroic exploits of a host of Elizabethan sea-dogs whose efforts laid the foundation for Britain's world-wide empire. The years 1558-1603 were accorded the status of a 'golden age' because they were thought to be such a contrast with the preceding and the following periods. Elizabeth was claimed to have built a strong and stable regime, and in so-doing to have rescued the country from the 'mid-Tudor crisis'. This was presented as being a period of political turmoil and incipient civil strife covering the final years of Henry VIII's reign (from about 1540 to 1547) and the reigns of his son, Edward VI (1547-53), and of his elder daughter, Mary (1553-8). It was said that after Elizabeth's death England temporarily reverted to its former state of political instability when, under the early Stuarts (James I and Charles I), it stumbled into discord, civil war, and the collapse of the monarchy. It is little wonder that the time of 'Good Queen Bess' seemed to shine out as a beacon - an era of greatness, promising even better things to come.

The adulation of Elizabeth I and of the achievements of her age reached its height in the early-1950s when for a second time a young woman named Elizabeth ascended her nation's throne. There was much optimistic talk, sometimes reflecting a state of near euphoria, and the promise was held out of the dawn of a 'new Elizabethan age' when, presumably, past greatnesses would be repeated. Popularising historians such as A.L. Rowse captured the mood of the times with their eulogistic descriptions of late-sixteenth-century England and two major academic historians - J.E. Neale (later, Sir John - he was knighted in recognition of his services to history) and Conyers Read - completed their lifetimes' work on the political history of the first Elizabeth's reign. It seemed that Elizabeth Tudor's reputation as one of England's greatest leaders had been so firmly established that it would remain unassailed for all time.

However, by 1960 interest in the Elizabethan age had all but faded away. It had become clear that the accession of the second Elizabeth had not signalled a national revival. In fact, it was apparent that just the opposite was happening and that national decline was gathering pace. There was no doubt that the British economy was falling further behind its rivals and that the country's status as a major world power was becoming more and more questionable. The Suez fiasco of 1956 had revealed how limited was Britain's ability to act independently of the USA, and it was obvious that the Empire was in a seemingly irreversible state of disintegration. Pessimism had replaced optimism as the order of the day. This change in public mood reinforced the existing inclination of political historians to turn their attention to periods other than 1558-1603. This was partly because it looked as if all the worthwhile work on the Elizabethan age had already been done by Neale and Read, but it was also partly because lively debate was taking place about the periods before and after the reign of Elizabeth I. The controversies over Elton's 'revolution in Tudor government' and the nature of the mid-Tudor crisis were gathering pace, while exciting new approaches to the study of the 'English Revolution' of the mid-seventeenth century were being pioneered. Quite naturally, research historians were drawn to where the action was.

For about twenty years the situation remained much the same. Then research findings began to appear which suggested that the 'old orthodoxy' primarily established by Neale and Read was not as watertight as had been thought. By 1984 enough new work had been done to allow Christopher Haigh, possibly the most able of the new generation of researchers working on Elizabethan history, to gather together a collection of essays (*The Age of Elizabeth*) which questioned various aspects of the established interpretations. The efforts of these 'revisionist' historians (as they are called) have produced a number of striking results. Some aspects of the 'old orthodoxy' have been totally demolished, while others have been shown to require significant modification. And the work continues, so it would be dangerous to imagine that any of the currently accepted interpretations are written on tablets of stone. This is why so many of the conclusions reached in the chapters that follow will appear somewhat tentative. It is also the reason why students writing about the politics of Elizabethan England would be well advised to get into the habit of including qualifying words such as 'possibly', 'probably', and 'likely' in the judgements they make.

Although the work of the revisionists has not yet come together to form a coherent new interpretation of the political history of the later sixteenth century, it has led to a re-evaluation of the part played by Elizabeth herself. All of those who have challenged aspects of the old orthodoxy would agree that the picture traditionally presented of the queen has been far too laudatory and uncritical - that her successes have been exaggerated and her shortcomings minimised. However, this is not to suggest that there is any agreement about what the new assessment of Elizabeth as queen should be. There is no consensus about either the aspects of Elizabeth's performance that should be evaluated afresh or the extent to which her achievements should be 'downgraded'. It is therefore left to each student of this topic to make provisional judgements about Elizabeth's quality as a queen. This is the central task with which this volume attempts to assist you. By the time you finish reading it and thinking about what you have read you should be in a position to present your own opinions about Elizabeth's strengths and weaknesses as the ruler of England between 1558 and 1603. But because this book does not cover all aspects of the political history of Elizabeth's reign you will need to test out the conclusions you reach against the evidence you collect from elsewhere. John Warren's *Elizabeth I: Religion and Foreign Policy* in this series has been designed to complement the current volume in this respect.

Two aspects of Elizabethan politics have received special attention from revisionist historians. The queen's dealings with parliament have been very carefully scrutinised. This has happened because one of the first revisionist 'break-throughs' was the discovery of flaws in the highly respected orthodox interpretation of the topic. This had been made by J.E. Neale in his two-volume account of the relations between Elizabeth and her parliaments which had been published in the 1950s. Once it became clear that the weaknesses in Neale's case were right at the heart of his interpretation, it was not long before the credibility of his central contention was destroyed. This has been such a major event in the study of the political history of the period that the issue has had an entire chapter devoted to it. A second issue has been singled out for similar treatment. This is the question of the significance of Elizabeth's final years. Here the revisionist thrust has been neither as incisive nor as coherent as over the issue of parliament, but nonetheless it has been of considerable importance. However, given the current state of the debate, it presents greater difficulties for the student. So much uncertainty surrounds the issue that any conclusions reached must be couched very tentatively indeed.

The same is true of two other issues that have been separated out for treatment on their own - the way in which the questions of Elizabeth's marriage and the succession were handled, and the relationship between Elizabeth and her leading servants. In both cases the issues have been isolated because they have a coherence of their own rather than because they have been the subject of notable attention by revisionist historians. This distinction will be apparent from the structure of the chapters in question. In each of them the framework is provided by historical aspects of the issue rather than by the differing interpretations advanced by historians, as is the case with the two chapters referred to in the previous paragraph.

Of course, not all historical interest in the politics of the period 1558-1603 has focused on the activities of Elizabeth I. Other figures have rightly been thought to be of significance. There are at least a dozen people (all men) who could be considered to fall within this category. Of these, only three - Sir William Cecil (Lord Burghley), the Earl of Leicester, and the Earl of Essex - have received independent treatment within this volume. In each case they have been selected for inclusion primarily because their activities were so intertwined with those of the queen that some appreciation of their political careers is essential if anything approaching a balanced evaluation of Elizabeth's performance is to be made. It is hoped that - especially with Cecil and Leicester - the coverage has been sufficiently detailed for an assessment to be made of each man's contribution to the political life of the nation.

Studying *'Elizabeth I and the Government of England'*

This book has been designed so that, if necessary, each of the following six chapters can be studied in isolation. This has been done so that the needs of those who are 'targeting' particular aspects of the politics of Elizabeth's reign will be met. However, it is undoubtedly the case that much of the benefit of using this volume is only likely to be gained by those who study it as a whole.

It is strongly recommended that once the entire book has been read this brief introduction is studied again and a conscious check is made that each of its points has been understood. Then will be the time to undertake the task that will pull together all the separate pieces of work that have been done - making an overall assessment of Elizabeth's performance as a monarch. There are many effective ways of doing this. Most of them involve going through the notes you have made and extracting relevant evidence to be included in lists of points 'for' and 'against'. If you are able to think through the process of evaluation in abstract terms you will be able to select various sets of criteria according to which to make your judgements. For example, you may decide to make lists of advantages and disadvantages - situations over which Elizabeth had no control, such as her gender and the duration of her reign. You may also opt for headings such as 'strengths' and 'weaknesses' or 'successes' and 'failures'. It certainly would be helpful to make more than one set of lists if you can. You should find that many items appear in both lists under any pair of headings, which is hardly surprising as most characteristics have a plus and a minus side depending on the situation. When you have made your lists you need to weigh one against the other. Although it would be surprising if you decided that Elizabeth had more minuses than pluses as a queen - even the most radical revisionist would accept that on balance she was good at her job - it is for you to judge whether she was 'good', 'very good', or 'excellent', and why. This is the main task that the following chapters are designed to assist you in doing.

CHAPTER 2

Elizabeth I

Any understanding of the political history of the reign of Elizabeth I must be based on a clear appreciation of the character and personality of the queen herself. This is because Elizabeth played a crucial part, either directly or indirectly, in almost every aspect of public life in England between 1558 and 1603. Either she made the decisions herself or she greatly influenced those who did. The monarch was the political power in the land in almost all senses of the term. Most of those who played an active part in the government of her kingdom consciously attempted to please her, while only the extremely foolhardy risked doing anything that would arouse her anger towards them.

1 A Formidable Person

Clearly Elizabeth was a formidable person. In part this was a consequence of her considerable intellectual ability. There has been unanimous agreement among commentators that she was very clever, and none of them have expressed surprise that this was so. After all, both her mother (Anne Boleyn) and her father (Henry VIII) were among the most academically gifted people of their generation. Elizabeth's brain power was displayed from an early age. By the time she had reached her early teens she had mastered Latin sufficiently well to be able to read, write and speak it with confidence, although the customary expectation of 'maidenly modesty' led her to pretend that she was less good than she really was. In addition, she was already proficient in French and Italian and was soon to acquire sufficient command of Greek to be able to read it with little difficulty. The process of learning Latin involved developing the abilities to marshal ideas in a coherent way at great speed and to expound them orally or in writing with a high degree of elegance (according to the tastes of the time which were copied from those of classical Rome). Elizabeth exercised and further developed these skills throughout her life, to the considerable wonderment of the many witnesses (English and foreign) who reported examples of her using them to great effect. She generally cloaked her pride in her academic accomplishments with extravagant, but false, displays of modesty - which of course only served to impress her audiences even more - although the mask was allowed to slip somewhat when, in her early sixties, she went to elaborate lengths to establish that she had just translated one of the Latin classics into English in record time, outdoing King Alfred among many others! But, of course, it was the daily use to which she put her highly trained mind that contributed so much to Elizabeth's effectiveness as a monarch. She tore to shreds any poorly reasoned argument that was presented to her and, in the process, ensured that rarely were any but the most carefully devised plans of action presented to her for approval. Those who wished to remain in her service went to great lengths to avoid careless work and sloppy thinking. They were constantly 'on their toes' because they knew that their mistress was sure to catch them out if they were not. Even the most efficient of her administrators, Sir Robert Cecil, was frequently in a state of high anxiety, fearing that his work would be found to be unsatisfactory.

Of course, intellect alone would not have been sufficient to make Elizabeth a formidable person. An equally important attribute was her unshakable self-confidence. From the moment she became queen at the age of 25 until she died 45 years later she was completely convinced that she was the foremost person in her domains. Her belief that she was God's representative on earth, as far as her dealings with her subjects were concerned, was deep and abiding. She did not, even for one moment, imagine that there could be any constraint, besides her own conscience, placed on her actions, and she was well aware that her habit of operating within the law (rather than above it) was a matter of choice rather than of necessity. But her self-assurance never took the form of arrogance. She was very matter-of-fact about her 'superiority', sometimes bemoaning the fact that an accident of birth (she was careful to claim no credit for the position in which she found herself) had loaded so many cares and responsibilities on her. She is reported several times as saying that had she been born a simple milk-maid life would have been better for her. As a result of her certainty about the relative importance of the position she held she rapidly came, as queen, to adopt a bearing of natural authority. This led her subjects, high and low, to act towards her on almost all occasions with the extreme deference that she so patently expected of them. Those who chose in rare informal situations to treat her virtually as an equal needed to be very sure of the personal love and affection in which they were held. But even her favourites could misjudge what was acceptable. In the 1590s the Earl of Essex was excused for taking many liberties but even he was to find that Elizabeth's personal love of him did not always determine her actions as queen. Not only were his ears soundly boxed for crudely telling his monarch what he thought of her, but in 1601 he even paid with his life for daring to attempt to intimidate Elizabeth by a show of force (see page 131).

Not only did Elizabeth know in detail how she expected to be treated, but she was consistently determined that her standards should be met. 'Forgive and forget' was not a part of her nature. On occasions she did relent when someone had offended her, but such 'softness' was the exception to the rule. Normally a first mistake was a last mistake, as the blighted lives of a long list of disgraced servants (humble and aristocratic alike), officials, courtiers and distant relatives bore witness. Her special favourites often found their way back into her good books after an upset, although the penance exacted for their misdemeanours was sometimes long and arduous, but few others rose again once they had fallen. For many only death (normally a natural one) brought an end to royal disfavour once it had been acquired. Whether actions are judged to be the result of determination (a virtue) or stubbornness (a defect) often depends on the perspective of the observer. But, whatever label is chosen, it is clear that Elizabeth's consistency of attitude over both people and policy contributed significantly to her formidableness.

2 Elizabeth's Popularity

Although some recent research has raised doubts about the universality of the queen's popularity, it seems certain that the traditional picture of 'Good Queen Bess' has a large element of truth to it. Elizabeth was probably the most popular monarch in British history. This judgement can be maintained despite the fact that an amount of the evidence that has normally been used to support it dates from the second decade of the seventeenth century when writers were extolling the 'good old days' as a way of obliquely (and therefore safely) drawing attention to the unpopularity of James I, and is therefore not greatly to be trusted. It is also a view that can be supported even though there is ample evidence that in the final decades of Elizabeth's reign a sophisticated royal propaganda machine was in operation aimed at maintaining the belief that popular adulation of the ageing monarch was widespread and intense. However, when the effects of these two factors are stripped away the evidence of the esteem in which Elizabeth was held by the people of England remains impressive. It is just possible (but unlikely) that future research will result in a plausible case being established that much of the queen's apparent popularity was created by Protestant writers who used the last of the Tudors as a focus for mass loyalty and affection in an effort to weaken the lingering influence of Catholicism on the hearts of the people at large. Certainly the basis for such a contention already exists, but there is so much independent evidence which appears to emanate from unbiased sources that it is almost unimaginable that more than a small fraction of it could ever be discredited.

What is perhaps surprising is that Elizabeth's popularity was apparent even when she was a young woman, and before she ascended the throne. During Mary's reign crowds gathered to greet the heir apparent wherever she went, to wish her well, and to present her with whatever little gifts could be afforded. The same pattern appears to have occurred for the rest of her life, although the spontaneity was often missing in later years because of the careful stage-managing that went on. However, despite the formality and artificiality of much of the queen's contact with her people from the 1570s onwards, there are plenty of examples of positive popular feelings breaking through. There remain reports written by 'ordinary' people after seeing the queen in which the enthusiasm expressed seems not to have been merely the result of effective image-making, but rather to reflect feelings of loyalty and respect which would have been present even had the propagandists not been at work. It seems safe to conclude that Elizabeth was a genuinely popular monarch, even though it must be conceded that that popularity was certainly enhanced by those whose purpose was to put her forward in the best possible light.

The majority of the propagandists who sought to extol Elizabeth were self-appointed and were in no sense official. The publicity campaign began from the moment Queen Mary died. As Elizabeth made her way through the streets of London on the day of her accession she encountered carefully contrived *tableaux* (static displays by actors presenting well-known stories or making a political point - rather like a living cartoon) in which she was portrayed as the restorer of true religion and the scourge of false prophets. Clearly the Protestants who arranged for these flattering displays had at least two aims in mind. They hoped to whip up support for the new queen, but they also intended to apply pressure on her to introduce the type of religious changes which they favoured. Almost the whole of the flood of pro-Elizabeth Protestant propaganda which continued throughout her reign - whether it took the form of printed books, pamphlets, broadsheets and woodcuts or dramatic presentations in the form of plays, interludes and *tableaux* - was designed to influence policy as well as to glorify the queen. However, the policy to be advocated changed with the passage of years for, as it became clear that Elizabeth was determined to maintain the Church on a Protestant path, the need to reinforce her Protestant resolve at home grew less and the attempt was made to persuade her to become the saviour of international Protestantism, especially by assisting the Dutch rebels in the Netherlands in their attempt to free themselves from their Spanish Catholic ruler. There is no doubt that as more and more Englishmen came to think of themselves as Protestants the constant portrayal of Elizabeth as the sole effective protector of their religion, whether at home or abroad, greatly enhanced the stature of the queen in the eyes of the population as a whole.

The second major thrust of the propaganda effort to enhance Elizabeth's popularity was the portrayal of her as her country's foremost servant as well as its God-given ruler. In the second half of her reign, especially when it became clear that she would never marry, she was proudly referred to (and referred to herself) as the 'Virgin Queen'. This was an expansion on the idea which she had first formulated in her twenties that she was content (even honoured) to act as if she had taken England as her husband and was devoting herself entirely to its service. This was a novel and imaginative stance to take and seems to have been formulated by Elizabeth herself. Perhaps she thought of it by a piece of lateral thinking, working from the standard argument used by the Catholic Church that monks, nuns and priests should remain celibate because they were already married to God. Whatever its origins, it was certainly a very effective metaphor. There were very few subjects who were not flattered to receive such expressions of devotion from their sovereign. Even though the concept of the Englishman's 'stiff upper lip' had not been thought of when Elizabeth was queen, (it was a nineteenth century invention), it is still noteworthy that grown men are reported as having been moved to tears whenever a version of the 'Virgin Queen' speech was made.

It is clear that Elizabeth's widespread popularity was partly of others' making and partly a result of circumstances beyond her control - especially the fact that Protestants had so much hope vested in her after the reign of Mary had seemed to spell the ruin of their cause - but it is equally certain that she deserves much of the credit for the esteem in which her subjects generally held her. A critic might say that she unashamedly 'milked' every situation when she was in the public's view for all it was worth, while a supporter might choose to draw attention to the fact that she missed no opportunity to be seen by her people and to be heard saying what it pleased them to be told. She was undoubtedly an adroit showman from a young age and she certainly liked to be liked. Whereas it would have been reasonable for her to travel in as much privacy as the rudimentary facilities of the time allowed, she always insisted on being literally on view as much as possible. Crowds were seen as a reason to stop and be greeted rather than as a potential inconvenience or danger to be hurried past with a minimum of delay. Boring and over-long speeches of welcome were listened to with a good grace when perhaps they deserved to be cut short, and immense care was taken to ensure that her appearance was always appropriate to the occasion. The summer progresses during which she journeyed around the southern shires of her kingdom for several months in most years of her reign (they were sometimes cancelled as an economy measure, despite the fact that she stayed at the residences of leading subjects and at their expense!) were utilised as opportunities to be seen by as many people as cared to line her pre-publicised routes, and as occasions on which she could dispense small gifts and minor favours as liberally as possible. If walk-abouts had been thought of at the time Elizabeth would undoubtedly have utilised them! Given that the queen was seen as being no more responsible for the people's ills than modern members of the royal family are, it is little wonder that she was generally judged by the public image she presented rather than by the economic circumstances of the time or by the policies that were being pursued (as would probably be the case with a current politician). No English monarch before Elizabeth had courted popularity so overtly or so persistently. This, together with the skill with which she conducted herself in public, explains why she was the object of more popular affection than any of her predecessors and almost all of her successors.

One incident exemplifies Elizabeth's approach to maintaining her popularity. In 1588 it was widely and correctly predicted that Spanish forces from the Netherlands in combination with a large fleet of warships from Spain (the Armada) were preparing to mount an invasion of southern England in an attempt to dethrone the queen and to replace her with a Catholic. Once the Armada had been sighted off the Cornish coast and public anxiety was at its height, Elizabeth insisted on joining the army that had been stationed at Tilbury (in Kent) in order to head off any attack on London. She gave instructions for the soldiers to be drawn up ready for her to address them. She appeared splendidly attired in partial armour and delivered the following speech:

1 My loving people, we have been persuaded [by those] that are careful of our safety, to take heed how we commit ourselves to armed multitudes, for fear of treachery. But I assure you, I do not desire to live to distrust my faithful and loving people. Let tyrants
5 fear ... I have always so behaved myself that, under God, I have placed my chiefest strength and safeguard in the loyal hearts and good will of my subjects, and therefore I am come amongst you as you see at this time, not for my recreation and disport, but being resolved, in the midst and heat of the battle, to live or die amongst
10 you all, to lay down for my God, and for my kingdom, and for my people, my honour and my blood, even in the dust. I know I have the body of a weak and feeble woman, but I have the heart and stomach of a king, and of a king of England too, and think foul scorn that Paramour Spain or any prince of Europe should dare to
15 invade the borders of my realm, to which, rather than any dishonour shall grow by me, I myself will take up arms, I myself will be your general, judge and rewarder of every one of your virtues in the field. I know already for your forwardness you have deserved rewards and crowns, and we do assure you, in the word of
20 a prince, they shall be duly paid you ... By your valour in the field, we shall shortly have a famous victory over these enemies of my God, of my kingdom and of my people.

Because she was aware that many of those present could not hear her words, Elizabeth arranged for a copy of her speech (handwritten by her clerks) to be given to the captain of each company of soldiers so that he could read it to his men that evening. They would not have known that the queen had returned to London by then! However, it should not be concluded that the speech was merely a piece of public relations duplicity. Elizabeth undoubtedly believed in and meant the spirit of what she said even though she, and the vast majority of her audience, understood that the words were not always to be taken literally. It seems that the genuineness of the sentiments she expressed was readily accepted by those who heard her.

A second example of Elizabeth's technique might help to explain her success in dealing with her ordinary subjects. It was customary for the crowds that gathered to see her to shout 'God save the queen' when she appeared. But rather than just accepting this acclamation with a wave of her hand as would have been reasonable (and as Henry VIII regularly had done), Elizabeth normally responded with the words 'God bless you all, my good people'. This simple gesture of good will was reported with enthusiasm by observer after observer, and there is no doubt that it helped to create what some modern-day popular psychologists would term 'a positive feel-good situation'. It was symptomatic of the queen's attention to the detail of fostering good relations with her subjects.

3 Elizabeth's Statecraft

It used to be thought that Elizabeth was outstanding at the day-to-day work of being her country's leader. This was the judgement normally made during the first century or so of the large-scale academic study of history in Britain (up to the 1950s), when it became the received wisdom that the late sixteenth century was a 'golden age' in England's past. In recent decades the adulatory tone employed by earlier writers when describing Elizabeth's part in the government of the country has largely been missing. It is not that the old orthodoxy has been turned on its head but rather that the praise has been more restrained and that the queen's shortcomings have been highlighted more often.

However, it is still possible to identify aspects of considerable skill in Elizabeth's conduct of affairs as England's monarch. The most widely accepted of her strengths is that she was very good at selecting the men on whom she would rely to carry out the detailed work of government. In addition, it is generally agreed that she showed good judgement in standing by her leading servants even when things were not going well - Henry VIII's soon-to-be-regretted desertions of Cardinal Wolsey and Thomas Cromwell stand out in stark contrast. By far the most notable of her chosen men was Sir William Cecil (Lord Burghley from 1571). His loyalty and devotion to his queen could not have been greater and the efficiency of his administration was of a high order. He was one of the outstanding royal ministers - although he was solid rather than inspirational - of the early modern period, and Elizabeth did well to recognise his worth and to utilise his services as extensively as she did. At times she also displayed great resolve by resisting intense pressure to dismiss him.

It has also been widely noted that Elizabeth helped to maintain good order in public affairs by making judgements according to the merits of the case rather than being swayed by her feelings towards the individuals who advocated the different possible courses of action. Thus the fact that one of her favourites - even if she was in love with him at the time - pressed her to follow a particular policy did not make it any more likely that her decision would be as he wished it to be. The determination that she frequently showed in the face of the pleadings or sulkings of her politically-thwarted favourites has aroused considerable admiration among many of her biographers. This trait was particularly in evidence in her dealings with the Earl of Leicester during the 1560s and 1570s (see page 66). However, it appears that this strength of resolve did not remain throughout her life. It has been argued quite convincingly that she weakened considerably in this respect during the final decade of her reign (see page 129).

Other aspects of Elizabeth's dealings with those who were close to her (either physically or emotionally) have generally continued to be commented on favourably. It is not just rulers of countries who face potential difficulties in controlling those who regulate the access of people and information to them: it is a problem for anybody in a position of major responsibility in a large organisation. Nowadays there are well-publicised strategies for overcoming most of the difficulties associated with this situation, but in the sixteenth century (and later) these had not been developed. Therefore Elizabeth had to chart her own course through a potential minefield of manipulation and special pleading. On the whole she did this with considerable skill. Her strategy was simple. She made it difficult for people to influence her via those who attended her day-by-day by making it clear to these 'servants' (the members of her Privy Chamber, most of whom were well-bred and with important political connections) that she would not be pleased if she discovered that any of them were attempting to promote special interests by telling her some things and hiding others from her. When one of the people close to her - normally it was a lady-in-waiting - was unwise enough not to heed the warning the result was a violent verbal assault at the least, (Elizabeth administered these so effectively that few risked laying themselves open to such an attack on a second occasion), and a spell, of unspecified length, in the Tower of London at the worst. As far as can be judged from the surviving evidence, it seems that the queen was as successful as she reasonably could have been at keeping her household 'non-political'.

Sometimes the attempts made to manipulate the flow of people and information to Elizabeth were part of a strategy aimed at influencing government policy, but more frequently the intention was to influence a decision on a question of patronage. Patronage took a wide variety of forms, covering the making of any appointment or grant that was in the monarch's gift. These appointments or grants usually resulted in financial gain ranging from a few tens of pounds to thousands of pounds per year for the recipient. They were the 'pay-offs' that most courtiers and their dependants expected in return for devoting their lives to the service of their monarch. A minority of patronage decisions affected status or political power rather than income (the award of titles and appointment to bodies such as the Privy Council are the most striking examples) and these were sometimes vied for even more energetically than those that had merely to do with money (see page 29 for a fuller discussion of patronage).

It was for a long time the custom among historians to enthuse over the queen's handling of patronage. In particular, it was judged that she showed outstanding political wisdom in ensuring that the gifts she had to bestow were distributed evenly so that no one faction (the followers of a leading political figure) was allowed to gain control of the flow of gifts and honours. This was thought to be important in ensuring the existence and the continuation of a 'balance of power' within political circles, whereby the members of no group saw themselves as losers and therefore as needing to take extreme action to redress the situation. It became the norm to contrast the situation under the last of the Tudors with that under the first two Stuarts. Elizabeth was seen as keeping the ship of state in calm waters by utilising patronage to minimise discontent among the political classes, while James I and Charles I were criticised as being inept in that they unnecessarily alienated many of their leading subjects by allowing the Duke of Buckingham virtually to monopolise the flow of patronage. It has often been claimed that they thereby contributed significantly to the causes of the Civil War.

However, in recent decades such an analysis has become unfashionable. This is because perceptions on three issues have changed noticeably. Firstly, it used to be stressed that the long-term causes of the Civil War which started in 1642 were very important. This meant that the events of the first decades of Stuart rule were accorded considerable significance and that the contrast between the skilful handling of matters by Elizabeth and the clumsiness of James I and Charles I was often highlighted. However, since the 1980s historians studying the seventeenth century have concluded that it is the short-term causes of the Civil War that mattered most and, as a result, Elizabeth's handling of the political situation during her reign has tended to be made less of. Secondly, as will be discussed in chapter 7, it has been argued increasingly strongly that the queen's touch was much less sure during the final decade of her reign when patronage was allowed to become a disruptive issue, leading to the abortive coup of the Earl of Essex in 1601. Thirdly, there has been a strong challenge to the old orthodoxy that in the 1560s and 1570s there was almost an undeclared war between the Cecil and Leicester factions which was only kept in hand by the skilful handling of Elizabeth. It has been claimed that Cecil and Leicester worked together as often as they competed with one another and that factionalism was much less significant than used to be thought. It therefore follows that the queen can no longer be given great praise for averting a crisis that never really existed.

Thus recent assessments of Elizabeth's political skills have tended to be more 'down-beat' than they used to be. Whereas she used to be regarded as an outstanding practitioner of statecraft, it is now generally agreed that such judgements exaggerated her abilities. At the same time, more attention has been focused on her shortcomings than used to be the case.

4 Elizabeth's Shortcomings

Elizabeth was a most frustrating monarch to serve. It is said that she would have tried the patience of a saint. Her almost pathological dislike of making decisions was her most discomfiting trait. The fact that she was consistent in this habit throughout her reign did not make the situation any easier for her ministers and officials to cope with. No-one discovered a workable method of circumventing it, and its very predictability made it no less aggravating, especially for those whose work was seriously inconvenienced or whose efforts were totally wrecked by their inability to secure a decision at the necessary time. Persistence, patience, petulance and 'jollying along' were all found to be equally useless as techniques for persuading the queen to give a definite answer. Those who displayed little skill in manipulating her were normally dismissed having been given the impression that she would think about it. Those whose influence with her was greater could often secure a promise that she would decide 'soon' or even 'tomorrow' - only to find that the next day brought forth further excuses for delay. The really influential, such as Cecil or her favourite of the moment, could often secure a signature at a first or second attempt, but this was frequently followed within minutes by a message that she had changed her mind. In the circumstances it is hardly surprising that those seeking a decision often arranged for a courier to be standing by so that a signed document could be hurried away beyond recall if the need arose!

The rapid changes of mind, allied to the extreme reluctance to decide one way or the other on most matters, would have speedily resulted in a paralysis of government in a modern state. However, in sixteenth-century England the consequences were not catastrophic. This was because in most respects the life of the nation continued unaffected even if there was a haemorrhaging of decision-making in central government. Frequently the only people affected by such a situation were those in the court circle itself. It is true that foreign policy issues could be adversely affected by monarchical indecision (this dimension is explored in John Warren's *Elizabeth I: Religion and Foreign Affairs* in this series) but even such matters impinged little on the everyday lives of most people. In fact, in a perverse way, Elizabeth's great weakness could sometimes turn out to be a strength. Given that any decision made by the queen was likely to disappoint more people than it pleased, there was often a greater chance of creating discontent by acting than by doing nothing. If, for example, several people had hopes of securing appointment to a particular office, Elizabeth's delaying of a decision caused great frustration but at least it kept alive the expectations of all. And this situation could be extended almost *ad infinitum*. It was not unusual for positions to be left vacant for several years, and in extreme cases appointments were only made decades after the promise to do so had originally been given.

Yet it would be misleading to give the impression that the queen's reluctance to make decisions was matter of little consequence. The 'drift' in government to which this gave rise meant that things that should have been done were left undone. Even in a society as static as Elizabethan England there were developments over a period of time that needed to be mirrored by changes in either the structure or the policies of government, and not all of them were. Crown finances was the most obvious field in which governmental inactivity caused avoidable problems. The inflation that was such a feature of western European life in the sixteenth century was particularly marked in England during Elizabeth's reign. Action should have been taken, especially in respect of *ad valorem* customs duties (duties which were a stated percentage of the supposed value of the goods) and the rents payable on Crown lands, to reflect the rise in prices but virtually nothing was done. As a result, the queen's income from the sources of what was known as her 'ordinary revenue' was much lower than it might reasonably have been. This necessitated both the placing of strict limitations on government expenditure and the development of alternative (and normally unpopular) ways of raising money. Both strategies gave rise to problems that might have been avoided had decisive action been taken over the erosion of the real value of Crown income caused by inflation.

Another well-publicised shortcoming of Elizabeth's was her mean-ness. Her grandfather, Henry VII, had been 'careful with money' but he had been prepared to spend it to good effect when the situation called for lavishness. By way of contrast, the parting with money for almost any purpose seemed to cause Elizabeth pain. Not only did she sometimes deny those who loyally served her the rewards they justifiably expected, but she shied away from most policies, especially in foreign affairs, that threatened to involve her in avoidable expense. What is worse, when she did agree to other than routine expenditure, her parsimony often resulted in the project being less-well funded than it needed to be for success to be ensured. There were plentiful examples of those being given charge of enterprises having to dig deeply into their own pockets in an attempt to avoid a disaster that was in danger of being caused by a lack of resources. Unfortunately, such 'shoring-up' was often insuffi-cient to avert a calamity. This problem was apparent in virtually all the military and naval expeditions that were mounted during the reign.

Elizabeth was mean but she was not a miser. She disliked spending money, and especially she was averse to giving it away, but she showed no particular enthusiasm for acquiring it. Whereas Henry VII had worked doggedly to maximise his income, Elizabeth could not be persuaded to show a great deal of interest in any aspect of her financial affairs. One odd quirk of her attitude towards money was that she was prepared for her courtiers to enrich themselves, even if it was indirectly at her expense, as long as she did not have to part with money that had already come into her hands. Thus large profits were made by those to whom, for example, Crown lands were leased at well below current market prices, although in the process the queen was denied income she might otherwise have had. But the most politically damaging aspect of this strange attitude was Elizabeth's determination that wherever possible others (rather than she herself) should pay the price when she decided that one of her courtiers should be rewarded. Her technique was to grant the recipient a licence or a patent conferring some commercial privilege. The most notorious of these were patents awarding monopoly rights over the manufacture, sale, import or export of a particular product or commodity. This placed the patentee in a position to charge those who manufactured or traded in the goods a fee to carry on with their normal business. The result was that a courtier was enriched at the expense of the ordinary consumer who was forced to pay an artificially inflated price for what he or she purchased. By 1600 over 100 such patents (known as monopolies) had been granted, covering a wide variety of goods ranging from types of cloth to playing cards. The monopolies were, not unnaturally, greatly resented throughout the country. In the parliament of 1601 they were the cause of a considerable amount of ill-feeling between the queen and the House of Commons and it took all of Elizabeth's skills of pacification to damp down the passions that were aroused (see page 92). Nevertheless the discontent rumbled on, and it provided a significant part of the justification for those historians who have claimed that the reign ended on a very sour note. Although Elizabeth's meanness undoubtedly yielded some political advantages, especially in preventing her from amassing large debts that might have caused friction between herself and the political classes (at least if the experience of James I is anything to go by), it was primarily a weakness that made her less effective as a monarch than she otherwise would have been.

5 Explanations of Elizabeth's Personality and Character

Many of Elizabeth's numerous biographers have attempted to explain why her personality and character were as they were. It has generally been assumed that she inherited her intelligence and her determination from her parents and that her experiences as a child, an adolescent and a young woman did much to shape the characteristics she exhibited as queen. The implication has been that she did not change very much once she ascended the throne. There are good reasons to agree with this general analysis, although there is plenty of room for disagreement on specific issues. This will presumably always be the case. Modern professional psychologists researching the development of character and personality find it difficult to agree even when their 'subjects' are alive and available for detailed study, so there is little prospect of unanimity being reached about somebody who died 400 years ago and about whom the evidence is often tantalisingly partial. But then, for many people it is this in-built historical uncertainty that makes the study of the past so fascinating.

The bare facts of Elizabeth's early years make horrendous reading. When she was a toddler in her third year her mother (Anne Boleyn) was accused of multiple sexual misdemeanours, including sleeping with her own brother, was convicted of high treason, and was executed. Her father (Henry VIII) speedily remarried and at his insistence parliament disinherited Elizabeth and her elder sister Mary and declared them to be bastards. The young Lady Elizabeth, as she was still allowed to be called, was brought up in a small, tightly regulated, and poorly-funded household in the country. She was allowed almost no contact with her father, who showed virtually no interest in her or her welfare. He died when she was 13. A less propitious childhood for a future monarch could hardly be imagined.

However, it has normally been maintained that this catalogue of disadvantages was not nearly as harmful as might have been expected. The argument has been clear and convincing. Elizabeth, as was normal in royal circles at the time, was brought up by a titled governess and had very little to do with her parents. She would not have known of her mother's disgrace at the time it happened and would probably have been told about it in due course in such a way that both her parents appeared innocent. It seems reasonable to hypothesise that this was done by claiming that the evidence against Anne Boleyn had been fabricated and that Henry VIII had been grievously misled by wicked advisers. If this did happen, the young princess would probably not have thought it strange that her famous father was too busy to devote time to her. Nor would she have resented the fact that her brother Edward, although four years her junior, was the centre of attention. After all, in due course he would become king and would be her sovereign lord, while she was a mere female! On a day-to-day basis she was shown respect by those around her, and the fact that she was disinherited must have seemed of no importance to her as it in no way impinged on her life. She rapidly learned to take pride in being the daughter of the man who, she was told, was one of the world's great rulers, and her adoration of him was made easier by the fact that she knew little of the reality of the unpleasantly ageing monarch. Henry's death in 1547 must have been upsetting for her, but would not have been nearly as disturbing as it would have been had her father been significantly more than an 'image' to her. It seems that Elizabeth's childhood was psychologically relatively undamaging because, even if she was not shown great affection on a regular basis, she lived in a stable environment in which consistent values (hard work and respect for her male-betters) and beliefs (a Bible-based Protestant form of Christianity) were maintained - and were accepted by her.

In the final years of Henry's reign Elizabeth was very much taken under the wing of Queen Catherine Parr (Henry VIII's sixth and last wife). The two of them seem to have struck up a relationship based on mutual love and trust - one of the few such relationships Elizabeth was ever to experience. The closeness of former step-mother to former step-daughter continued even after Henry died and Catherine speedily remarried. It is generally agreed that it was under Catherine's influence that Elizabeth's commitment to Protestantism was consolidated. It is also the widely accepted view that it was while under Catherine's protection and control that the most formative experience of Elizabeth's adolescent years took place.

This occurred in 1548 when she was 14. Some of the details are disputed but the general picture of what happened is clear. At the centre of events was Lord Thomas Seymour, the younger brother of the Lord Protector, the Duke of Somerset. Both men enjoyed high status as uncles of the child king, Edward VI, (their dead sister, Jane Seymour, was his mother), but Thomas was openly discontented because he felt that his brother was monopolising the wealth and the power that should have been shared between them. The fact that he was rash, flamboyant, arrogant and unreliable prevented him from recognising that he was merely being treated according to his deserts. However, he was very personable and the sexually maturing Elizabeth developed a crush on him. Lord Thomas took advantage of the situation and let it be known that he was thinking of marrying the princess. For Somerset this was the final straw and he reluctantly allowed himself to be persuaded that his brother was becoming too dangerous to be allowed to live. Lord Thomas was arrested, accused of high treason, and executed. Elizabeth was interviewed in order to determine whether she had been party to the plotting. When it emerged that Lord Thomas had been allowed to take considerable liberties with the young princess - such as entering her chamber and tickling her while she lay in bed - it seemed that a circumstantial case against Elizabeth was being constructed. But those in power had nothing to gain from causing the downfall of the girl who was now recognised as second in line of succession to the throne, and Elizabeth's strenuous denials of any complicity in Lord Thomas's plans were accepted. The danger had passed but it had left its mark. Elizabeth realised how close to death her naivety had brought her and she determined to be much more vigilant in future. What was possibly a natural inclination towards caution now became an obsession. She developed the habit of looking and looking and looking again before she leapt. This way of behaving was to remain with her throughout her life - hence, most historians agree, her strong dislike of making decisions.

No doubt, many other experiences during the next few years played a part in forming Elizabeth's personality and character, but a lack of evidence means that we can only guess at what they were and what their impact was. For example, it seems reasonable to speculate that the death of Catherine Parr in childbirth might have had quite a marked effect, but we cannot know for certain. However, one well-documented episode does stand out as having scarred Elizabeth for life. It occurred in 1554 soon after Edward VI died and Mary became queen, when it was generally and correctly expected that a move would soon be made to return England to the Catholic fold after the official consolidation of Protestantism that had taken place during Edward's reign. Almost certainly unknown to Elizabeth, a group of prominent gentry laid plans to mount a rebellion against Mary with the aim of establishing a Protestant régime with Henry VIII's younger daughter as queen. This intention was announced in Kent by Sir Thomas Wyatt, the leader of the one 'arm' of the uprising that took place. Wyatt was defeated, arrested, and executed. Elizabeth, having heard of the way in which her name was being used, strenuously denied prior knowledge of what was intended and declared her unqualified loyalty to her sister. But it seemed that this would not be sufficient to save her. She was arrested in her turn, was refused the opportunity to justify herself in person before the queen, and was ordered to be detained in the Tower of London. Her panic-stricken entry to the Tower through the Traitors' Gate - a route reserved for those whose guilt was already assumed - provided one of the most dramatic and best documented (from several independent sources) moments of the Tudor period. For about two months Elizabeth lived with the constant expectation of an imminent announcement of her execution. But it never came. Instead, she was conveyed to an Oxfordshire manor house where she was kept under virtual house arrest for the remainder of Mary's reign. Although the immediate danger had soon passed, Elizabeth lived for several years with the knowledge that her increasingly suspicious and hostile sister might fatally turn against her at any moment.

Historians have identified a variety of ways in which this experience affected Elizabeth. First and foremost, it has been maintained that her already well-developed sense of caution was strongly reinforced both by the understanding that almost any of her actions could be misunderstood and by the appreciation that only by doing nothing could she be certain that she was not exposing herself to unnecessary risks. The consequences of this were to be felt for the rest of her life in her great dislike of making decisions. Secondly, it has frequently been argued, based on numerous references to her time in the Tower made by Elizabeth over many years, that the certainty that she was doomed, followed by a seemingly miraculous escape from her fate, convinced her that she was under God's special protection and that He had positively chosen her to be the instrument through which His will would be done on earth. This went a long way towards explaining both the strong (but uncomplicated) religious faith that Elizabeth exhibited throughout her reign and her unshakable certainty that the decisions she made as Supreme Governor of the Church of England were divinely inspired and therefore non-negotiable. Thirdly, it has been recognised that Elizabeth's unwillingness to sanction the execution of those 'near to the throne' (her attitude towards Mary, Queen of Scots, exemplifies this in its most extreme form) even when the evidence against them was compelling, almost certainly arose from her memories of what it was like to be an innocent person around whom a web of lies had been spun.

The cumulative effect of the large number of quasi-psychological explanations of Elizabeth's character and personality that have been published over the years has been to some extent to 'explain away' her shortcomings and to imply that she was not to blame for her weaknesses as a monarch. It is noticeable that a similar 'removal of responsibility' has not been presented for what have been perceived as being her strengths! This unintended consequence of the way in which Elizabeth's early life has been interpreted by historians has contributed to the aura of approval that overhangs almost all biographies of the Virgin Queen.

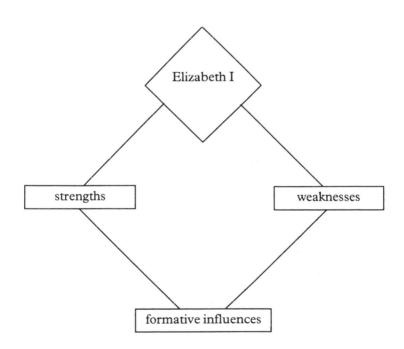

Summary - Elizabeth I

Making notes on 'Elizabeth I'

The aim of this chapter is to help you to acquire an understanding of those aspects of Elizabeth's abilities and attributes, and personality and character which particularly influenced her performance as Queen of England between 1558 and 1603.

You will need i) to identify what these were - they will provide the headings for your notes, ii) to explain each aspect in sufficient detail to show why (in what way and to what extent) it was important, and, iii) to make clear for each aspect what 'historical uncertainties' exist - where there is room for doubt or alternative interpretations. It would be helpful, although it is by no means essential, to note down your own opinions about why Elizabeth was as she was.

The notes you make at this stage are likely to be short of 'facts' - evidence and examples to substantiate the general points. That is because this chapter is designed to provide you with one framework within which you can organise your knowledge about the government of Elizabethan England. Many of the facts you need to 'put flesh on the bones' of this skeleton structure will be found in the later chapters of this book. So you would be well advised to leave good gaps between each section of your notes. This will allow you to add in the evidence on each point as you come across it.

Answering essay questions on 'Elizabeth I'

Most of the questions set about Elizabeth I require you to have much more knowledge than you have so far acquired - you would need to have read the rest of the book before being confident of being able to answer them successfully. However, it would be worth your while thinking about some possible titles at this stage so that you consciously identify a number of the issues to be kept in mind as you read the following chapters.

1   'Elizabeth I's skill as a ruler was largely as a man-manager.' Do you agree?
2   What advantages did Elizabeth I possess when she ascended the throne in 1558?
3   How far does Elizabeth I deserve the credit for the fact that England was so peaceful during her reign?
4   Assess the strengths and weaknesses of Elizabeth I as Queen of England.
5   Why was Elizabeth I so popular?

No doubt you will remember that one of the jobs to be done in the introductory paragraph(s) of an essay is to challenge assumptions made in the wording of a question if this is necessary. When answering two of the questions above it would be important to explore an assumption. Which are the questions that require this treatment, and what are the assumptions being made?

Look at question 2. It is a typical example of a straightforwardly worded direct question which most candidates will be attracted to answer. The majority of essays written will be descriptive lists with little to distinguish one from another. It will be difficult for the examiner to award such answers much more than an average grade. This is why simple questions are often said to be dangerous. What is needed is an approach that will allow some 'challenge' to be added to the question. A technique that often works is to adopt a plan that revolves around the fact that different historical interpretations would give different answers. In this case it would be done by saying that some commentators would describe a particular feature - for example, that Elizabeth was a woman - as an advantage while others would consider it to be a disadvantage. By outlining both sides of the argument and by indicating which side you favour and why you would be lifting your answer a long way above the ordinary.

Source-based questions on 'Elizabeth I'

1 Elizabeth's speech at Tilbury, 1588
Carefully read the extract from Elizabeth's speech, given on page 11. Answer the following questions.
a) Flattery was one of the techniques Elizabeth regularly used in her speeches. Explain why the technique was used. Give two examples of its use in this extract. (5 marks)
b) Elizabeth did not intend all her words to be taken literally. Quote an example from the extract and explain what message Elizabeth was intending to impart by speaking as she did. (5 marks)
c) What emotions was Elizabeth attempting to stir up in her audience? In each case justify your choice of emotion by reference to the extract. (6 marks)
d) What evidence is there that this performance was carefully stage-managed? (4 marks)

CHAPTER 3

Government and Politics

1 Introduction: Government

The chances are that when we think of the word 'government' we have in mind modern-day 'big' government. We are used to a situation in which the government's activities impinge on most aspects of our daily lives and are imagined to be responsible for most of the things that go wrong. There is disagreement about the detail of what our government should or should not do, but there is general agreement that it will be responsible for spending between a third and a half of all the wealth that is created in the country. Even those who argue for policies of low taxation and for people taking more responsibility for what happens in their lives find it difficult to conceive of a situation in which government spending will shrink dramatically.

Government in sixteenth-century England was something very different. It was extremely 'small'. For the vast majority of the population for most of the time it was just something that existed in the background. They knew that it was there but it was really not a concern of theirs. They rarely, if ever, paid any taxes (direct or indirect), and they expected no services to be provided for them. Two of today's biggest spending departments are education and social services (including health). In Elizabethan times these aspects of life were thought to fall outside the government's remit, and so nothing was spent on them from the public purse. So what was expected of the government? In as much as most people gave any thought to this - and most did not - the assumption was that its major role was to ensure the physical security of the country and of those who lived in it. On the one hand this meant that potential external attackers should be discouraged and that attempted invasions should be repulsed. But these 'national defence' issues were generally only of concern to those likely to be directly affected by foreign incursions - those in the southern coastal counties who, from time to time, feared an invasion from France or (towards the end of the century) from Spain, and the people of the far north who were perpetually apprehensive about possible raids from Scotland. On the other hand it had to do with the maintenance of law and order within the country so that the people's lives, livelihoods, and property (little though the majority possessed) were protected from destruction, disruption and theft. This was a constant concern in an age when violence was commonplace, when the strong took advantage of the weak (roving bands of 'sturdy beggars' featured strongly in popular imagination, although they were rarities in reality), and when natural disasters (especially flood and famine) were frequent occurrences. It was hoped that potential thieves and murderers would be dealt with before they became a problem, or, failing that, would be speedily apprehended and punished once their wrongdoings had been committed. It was also expected that action would be taken to maintain systems of drainage ahead of disasters and that plentiful supplies of food would be made available at reasonable prices in times of dearth.

It will be noticed that the concept of reform - the amendment of existing systems and the creation of new ones to cope with changing circumstances - was absent from the minds of most of the governed, as it was from the consciousness of those in positions of power. This was because modern ideas about progress - that 'things' will improve as time passes - were absent in Tudor times. People's aspirations were generally very limited. Their main hope was that things would not become too much worse. Conservatism, with a small 'c', was therefore the norm, and the natural response to any problem was to attempt to return things to how they used to be. One consequence of this situation was that those in authority were almost always 'reactive' rather than 'pro-active' - they tended to respond to what had already happened rather than attempting to take preventive action or employing avoidance techniques.

2 Introduction: Politics and Patronage

If a game of word associations was to be played with a group of present-day students, many of them would respond to 'government' with 'politics'. By this they would probably mean 'party politics'. This would not have been the case in the sixteenth century, when politics as we think of it today was unknown. There were no formally constituted political parties and there were none of the trappings of democracy (such as regularly contested elections, formal opposition, the presentation of alternative policies, and opinion polls) to which we have become used. Of course politics and politicians existed, although generally known by other names, but there were only a few similarities with those of today. At various times there were groups of influential people who shared a common policy objective and who co-operated together in an attempt to secure its implementation - the most notable example during Elizabeth's reign was the so-called 'Protestant party' which, during the 1570s and 1580s, championed intervention in the Netherlands in support of those rebelling against rule from Spain - and there were collections of individuals who could normally be relied upon to support the views of one of the leading public figures of the moment. However, the dissimilarities with our current situation were both more numerous and more significant.

Of greatest importance was the fact that those who played the game of politics - there were probably no more than about two and a half thousand of them at any one time - did so openly in the hope of personal gain. This was not corruption: it was what the game was all about. The gain could take several forms, the most clear-cut of which was financial. Almost without exception those who entered the political arena did so in the hope of securing some monetary reward. At the highest level, among those who aspired to be numbered among the queen's favourites, the sums of money involved could be very large. Both Lord Robert Dudley (Leicester) and Sir William Cecil (Burghley) joined the ranks of the richest men in the country as a result of the income they acquired from their political activities. Lesser figures could expect significantly to increase the income they received from other sources - by doubling it or even more - so the rewards were well worth seeking at all levels.

The most common way to secure an additional income was by being appointed to an official position for which a salary was payable. There were over a thousand of these and, in practice, they were generally held for life in that it was virtually impossible to dismiss a post holder once he had been appointed. Most of the positions had duties attached to them but they were rarely very onerous and, in any case, it was very common for a post holder to pay a fraction of the income he derived from the position to somebody else to deputise for him and to carry out the work required. At the lower end of the hierarchy of paid official positions it was not unusual for a post holder to employ a deputy in order to free himself to take on the role of deputy to a more highly paid official! This situation has made it even more difficult for historians to disentangle just what was happening. This has especially been the case when efforts have been made to calculate how much money particular post holders made from their official positions. A major complicating factor has been the right of many post holders to charge fees for work carried out by themselves or their deputy. These were often negotiated individually and were rarely recorded. In addition, many officials received 'presents' in cash and in kind from those who hoped to be treated favourably by them in the future, and/or hung on to government money that passed through their hands for much longer - sometimes for years, during which time they used it to their own advantage - than they should have done. Hence, estimates of the income derived from official positions have had to be tentative in the extreme.

The other ways of obtaining additional income from political activity were mainly restricted to those at the hub of government - the court circle. This was because the gains in each case tended to be large and could only be secured following a decision by the queen herself. Thus they were normally too valuable and too hard-won to be passed on to adherents in the country at large. All these sources of income shared one thing in common: they did not involve Elizabeth in spending money that she had already received. The fact that they led to her not receiving income which she otherwise might have done seems to have been less painful for her (see page 17). In dozens of separate arrangements, courtiers were made grants that allowed them to cream off part of the Crown's income. The queen was the largest landowner in the country. Her possessions were divided up into hundreds of different estates. Numbers of these were leased to courtiers at well below their market value, the recipients of the leases pocketing the difference between the rent they paid the queen and the rents they received from the tenants who farmed the estates. Another set of grants allowed particular courtiers to import or export a specified amount of a named commodity, such as cloth, without paying the normal customs duties. These grants or licences were then sold on to merchants who traded in these goods. Sometimes a courtier was allowed to buy the 'farm' of a particular commodity. By such arrangements a notional sum was paid to the Crown in return for the right to collect (and to keep) all the customs duties on the commodity in question. Such arrangements could be immensely lucrative. For example, in the 1590s the Earl of Essex depended for the majority of his income on the farm for the import of sweet wines. Equally eagerly sought were grants of wardship. These arose because by custom the queen was entitled to receive most of the income from the lands of her tenants-in-chief (those who, from feudal times, had held their estates directly from the Crown) if they were minors. Traditionally the monarch sold wardships as they arose to leading members of the court. During Elizabeth's reign the prices charged for wardships were normally only a fraction of their real worth, and some politicians, such as Sir William Cecil (Lord Burghley), made thousands of pounds from the wardships they purchased.

Some of the income acquired by politicians cost the queen nothing, either directly or indirectly. One technique amounted to nothing more than legalised robbery. Most new bishops, before their appointment was confirmed, had to agree to the leasing of some of the estates for which they were responsible and which made up the majority of the Church's remaining wealth (Henry VIII had seized most of the Church's property) to a leading courtier at well below their real value. Those churchmen who resisted the queen's 'requests' found that their promotions did not take place. Another approach was to grant a politician the sole right to bring prosecutions against those who infringed a particular act of parliament. This was of value to the recipient of the grant because those who 'laid the information' received a proportion of any fine levied. In practice, few cases ever came to court. Those who were ignoring legislation because it was in their financial interest to do so were normally prepared to buy off whoever had the sole right to bring a case against them. Quite naturally, neither the plundering of the Church nor the gathering of protection money from those who were flouting the law aroused much opposition other than from the few people who were directly affected. However, the third of the 'cost the Crown nothing' techniques aroused storms of protest. This was because most people felt they were out of pocket because of it. From the late-1570s onwards, but especially in the late-1590s, dozens of licences were granted allowing the patentee (the licences were granted by letters patent) the sole right to import, manufacture, or sell a particular commodity. These monopolies, as they were called, eventually spread to cover most items of everyday consumption. By 1600 it was jokingly (just) being suggested that bread would soon be added to the list. The monopolists made their money by charging the normal importers, manufacturers or retailers a fee to be allowed to carry on their trade. This 'rake-off' was, of course, passed on to the consumer. Hence the widespread unpopularity of the system. Monopolies are discussed at greater length on page 17.

Of course, not all the prizes that people sought to win by political activity were financial. Elizabethan England was a very hierarchical society in which most people believed that who you were was more important than what you had. Many people were more interested in improving their status than in acquiring additional possessions. Therefore the rewards that were most highly regarded were those that would enhance one's social standing, which money alone could not do. In court circles this was most frequently reflected in the complex scheming and (to us) childish squabbling that took place on a day-by-day basis. The aim was normally to win some sign of royal favour, especially if it were denied to one's competitors. Sometimes the goal was a more tangible one - the appointment to an honorific position or the award of a title. However, to hold such aspirations was an almost certain recipe for long-term anguish and frustration. Elizabeth was famed for her almost insuperable reluctance to grant such honours, and even the oft-repeated pleadings of her greatest favourites were rarely sufficient to move her. For example, when Elizabeth ascended the throne there were fewer than 60 peers in England and she had no intention of adding significantly to the number. Her belief was that nobility was something to which a person was born and that new titles, if they had to be created, should only be granted to those with noble blood in their veins. In keeping with these views, the number of new peerages that she allowed (10) was smaller than the number of existing titles that died out through lack of a male heir (12), and only one of these was granted to a man with a non-noble background (Sir William Cecil). Great favourites such as Christopher Hatton and Walter Ralegh were able to secure nothing more than knighthoods, but to gain even that was a rare distinction. Between 1558 and 1580 the number of knights declined from about 500 to about 300 because 'natural wastage' (knighthoods were not hereditary) so far outstripped new creations.

However, the leading politicians were successful in engineering an increase in the number of some prestigious positions. For the non-noble landowner of standing in his county community the accolade that was the surest sign of his prominence was to be appointed a Justice of the Peace (JP). Such appointments were made by the queen on an annual, but renewable, basis. So great was the clamour for inclusion in the list that, despite Elizabeth's known desire to keep the total number small, many counties ended the reign with twice as many JPs as they had had at the start of it. A less important, but nonetheless significant, sign of social standing was to be chosen as the member of parliament for a borough (being returned as a county MP - a knight of the shire - was highly prestigious and in practice was restricted to members of the leading few families in each county). Because there were always more aspirants than there were seats to be filled, leading courtiers consistently pressed for towns over which they exercised political control to be made into parliamentary boroughs so that they could reward more of their followers by having them returned as MPs. Such was the success of this pressure that during Elizabeth's reign the number of borough MPs was increased by 62. This was not a new trend - the queen was only responsible for about one third of the increase in the number of MPs that took place between 1500 and 1600 - but it was significant, as the size of the Commons grew by more than 10 per cent while Elizabeth was queen.

The process by which the rewards of politics were distributed in Elizabethan England is known as the patronage system. With thousands of appointments (paid and unpaid) to be fought over, there was a never-ending process of competitive jockeying for position going on. At the bottom of the 'pile' those with hopes of an initial piece of preferment formed a group of attention-seekers who waited on the rich and famous in order to make their mark in one way or other. Some of the saddest sixteenth-century figures of whom we know are those who devoted the best years of their lives to attempting to gain the patronage of a leading political figure but who, in the end, had nothing to show for their efforts. Of course, the fact that some, such as Christopher Hatton and Walter Ralegh, won through quite spectacularly persuaded many of the rest to keep trying. Presumably the psychology was the same as it is today for those who buy lottery tickets or do the pools. Higher up the scale were those who arrived well connected by birth or who had already made their way up several rungs of the political ladder. They had greater prospects of success but the competitive nature of the system meant that they had to devote most of their time and attention to developing a high profile if they were to make the progress they desired. Even those at the very top of the pyramid (for much of Elizabeth's reign Burghley and Leicester were the leading figures in the patronage system) had to work assiduously to maintain their dominant positions against potential rivals. Primarily this meant devoting themselves to ensuring that they remained in the queen's good graces, for it was from her that the major stream of patronage flowed. It was, of course, the fact that they enjoyed Elizabeth's special favour that allowed each of them to attract huge numbers of followers who hoped that their patron would be able to win them the objects of their desire. One indicator of the size of the patronage 'business' is the arrangements that Burghley made to cope with his share of it. He appointed a full-time patronage secretary to deal with the hundreds of letters he received each week seeking his support for some piece of personal advancement.

One of the strangest features of the patronage system to the modern eye is that ability and qualification played very little part in it. In the final analysis it was who you were and who you knew that mattered most. Of course, this was a reflection of the values and assumptions that governed Elizabethan society. Aspirations, such as fair play and equality of opportunity, that are often thought to epitomise the British way of doing things were not to become common currency until several centuries after Elizabeth's death, and some would argue that aspirations is all that they have ever been. But, however jaundiced a view one takes of the achievements of the liberal values that have dominated the last two centuries of life in Britain, it is clear that attitudes in Tudor England were very different from those of today. There was no embarrassment felt about - just as there was thought to be no need to justify - the fact that political activity was the process by which the few, especially those at court, sought to enrich themselves at others' expense. The view that 'to those that have shall be given' went almost totally unchallenged.

3 The Machinery of Central Government

The most noticeable thing about the machinery of central government in Elizabethan England was that there was so little of it. Although it is impossible to be precise, it seems that less than a thousand people (all men) carried out the government's work in London. The vast majority of them were involved in the state's two most sizable activities - finance and the law. Both were based on traditional systems that had grown up during the middle ages and were cumbersome and inefficient. However, they were highly respected by most prominent Englishmen, for whom the fact that they were of long standing was much more important than their shortcomings. Longevity of existence was generally thought to be a much more suitable criterion for judgement than fitness for purpose.

a) The Financial System

This ingrained conservatism is well illustrated by the history of the Crown's financial system in the hundred years from the mid-fifteenth century. The two Yorkist kings and their first two Tudor counterparts (Edward IV, Richard III, Henry VII and Henry VIII) largely broke free of the traditional ways of handling money via the clearly outdated Exchequer system. They established partially informal procedures within their households for dealing with the receipt, disbursement and auditing of their revenues - the money was kept in a large box in their private rooms. However, the Exchequer continued in existence, albeit with a much reduced role. But this was sufficient to provide the base from which the forces of reaction were able to capitalise on the absence of strong leadership during the reigns of Edward VI and Mary to undo many of the advances of the previous century by recapturing for the

Exchequer control of the Crown's income and expenditure. Although not all of the new and more efficient ways of dealing with business were abandoned, the dead hand of tradition was allowed to return the government's financial administration to its former obscurity. Once again, there was no way of knowing whether a surplus or a deficit was in prospect. In fact, summaries of accounts were rarely available until several years after the period to which they related. Those who handled the queen's money could play fast and loose with it safe in the knowledge that they would probably be able to delay giving an explanation of what they had done for a very long time.

b) The Legal System

The legal system shared many of the same attributes. In particular, it was based on ways of doing things that had been traditional since the middle ages. In fact, this continuity was considered to be its crowning glory, as custom lay at its very heart. Its principles were those of the common law, which was essentially a combination of ancient usage and the ways in which this had been interpreted in the past. It was argued that the concept of precedence was a more suitable guiding light for a legal system than the concept of justice because it depended on establishable fact rather than opinion. Although this approach had many advantages (primarily that it made corruption among judges virtually impossible to hide), it did have very obvious disadvantages. Most noticeably, it was very slow to adapt to changing circumstances. This was strikingly highlighted by the language in which the business of the main courts was conducted - the anglicised form of medieval French which had been the normal way of speaking among the élite in centuries past. This alone would have been enough to make the working of the law obscure to all but those who had received a lengthy training in it, even had it not been that an insistence on the detailed use of traditional procedures bemused everybody except experienced lawyers. Given this emphasis on precedence and long-established technicalities, it is hardly surprising that many cases were dismissed despite the fact that, in all justice, it should have been possible to proceed with them to a successful outcome. Very often the problem was that action being complained of was judged to fall outside the competence of the law because it neither exactly fitted the pattern of any previous case, nor was covered directly by any act of parliament. There could hardly be a clearer example of difficulties caused by the system's inability to deal with situations that it had not encountered before.

The three main common-law courts sat in the Palace of Westminster which was highly inconvenient for many of those who either wished or were compelled to attend them, even though it was almost exclusively the well-to-do (who were unlikely to suffer financial hardship by being made to travel to London) who had dealings with the law at this level.

However, because many serious criminal offences had to be tried in the county in which they had been committed, a number of judges were required to spend part of the year 'on circuit', travelling around the country hearing cases in temporary 'Crown Courts'. This provision did something to lessen the remoteness of the central legal system, although it could have done nothing to reduce most people's mystification at the way in which it operated.

Just as some of the inadequacies of the Exchequer system had been circumvented by establishing the royal household as an alternative centre of financial arrangements, so an effort had been made to redress some of the shortcomings of the common-law system by developing a rival set of courts. This had been possible because there was a firmly established tradition of the king's council acting as the arbiter in disputes between the more mighty subjects of the realm. The evidence is insufficient for us to be certain when and by what stages the 'prerogative' courts - so called because they relied for their authority on what were thought of as the God-given powers of the monarch (his prerogative) - came to prominence. But it seems that they were in effective operation by the end of Henry VII's reign and that they functioned extensively throughout the Tudor period. They continued their flourishing existence until the early-1640s when they were suppressed in the general attack that was made on the king's powers during the lead-up to the Civil War.

The most famous of the prerogative courts was the Court of Star Chamber, named after the star-shaped plaster mouldings on the ceiling of the room in Westminster Palace in which it habitually sat. This court heard tens of thousands of cases during Elizabeth's reign, all of which were brought to it by plaintiffs who chose to use it rather than becoming involved in the common-law system. This 'popularity' arose because Star Chamber, like the other prerogative courts such as the Court of Requests (which was intended for the use of people who could not afford the costs involved in bringing a case elsewhere), reached its verdicts on a basis of natural justice - the legal term was 'equity' - rather than of legal precedent, as happened in the common-law courts. The fact that a case was unlikely to be dismissed on a technicality and the prospect of lower costs which were made probable by the shorter time taken to try cases seem to have instilled confidence among those considering seeking legal redress for a wrong they had suffered. The speed of the prerogative courts was in part a consciously arrived at intention of those who championed the equity courts - they were keen to show up the proverbial slowness of the common-law courts - and in part the result of the fact that they did not need to spend large amounts of time considering past cases in order to establish precedents. As might be imagined, the equity courts were heartily detested by almost all the 500 or so common-law lawyers who were practising in London at any one time during Elizabeth's reign. This was partly based on self-interest, as they thought that each case heard in Star Chamber meant that there was less work available for them to do. But there were also matters of public concern at stake. Common-law lawyers argued that the justice dispensed by the equity courts was suspect because there was nothing to restrain the prejudices of those who made the judgements, as there was in the common-law courts. They maintained - it seems justifiably - that the procedures followed in Star Chamber often acted against the interests of defendants: hence, they claimed, the popularity of the prerogative courts among those who brought the cases. Some historians have seen the origins of the seventeenth-century legal profession's hostility to the powers of the Crown in the antagonism between the equity and common-law systems.

c) The Privy Council

The queen played almost no direct part in the workings of the financial and legal branches of central government. However, she was very much involved with the most dynamic and powerful element of the central government machinery - the Privy Council. She chose and dismissed its members, who served during her pleasure; she decided on its size and its working practices; she determined what issues it should consider and the extent to which it should be free to deal with them; and she made up her own mind whether or not to follow the advice it gave her. But she did not attend its meetings, and in practice she allowed it to carry on most of its business without any intervention from her. This was because much of its work related to humdrum administration. A high percentage of its time was devoted to considering and acting on reports about conditions (mainly religious and economic, but sometimes political) in various parts of the country. During a small proportion of sessions - but numerous in total, given that by the end of the reign meetings were held on every day of the week - issues of major political importance were discussed. This was normally done at the queen's specific request, although issues were sometimes raised when there had been no instruction to do so. However, such 'uninvited' forays were largely unproductive. The fact that Elizabeth had decided not to ask her councillors' advice on a matter almost invariably meant that her preference was to let things lie. So, when the Privy Council produced recommendations on the subject, it is little wonder that the queen's reaction was almost always very negative. Her emotional response varied between annoyance, anger, and fury, and her decision was predictable. She indicated that no action should be taken for the time being. This, of course, only added to the sense of frustration which had normally led to the councillors raising the issue in the first place. During the 1560s and 1570s the questions of what should be done about finding a husband for the queen, of the succession, of Mary, Queen of Scots' future, and of possible intervention in the Netherlands were fruitlessly aired in the

Privy Council on numbers of occasions. It seems that councillors regularly allowed themselves to be deceived into imagining that the queen would act differently on this occasion.

Thus the Privy Council was called upon to perform very disparate duties. It had to deal with administrative *minutiae* that would today be the responsibility of minor civil servants, while at the other extreme it spent time considering issues of the greatest national importance, directly bearing on matters of large-scale life or death and of war and peace. This range of activities made enormous demands on the skills of the councillors. They were required both to think large and to think small. A solid core could do this, but not all councillors were willing or able to do both. Therefore some members of the Privy Council were only very minor political figures, chosen because they would be able to conduct the details of business - especially dealings with other states - efficiently and with discretion. Others belonged to the small group of leading peers of the realm. Their inclusion was a reflection of the queen's need to be seen to be involving her magnates in major decisions of policy. At least, this was the situation in the first half of her reign. It says much about her growing confidence that for all but the last two years of the second half of her reign Elizabeth was content for there to be no senior members of the peerage on the Privy Council. During this period the number of councillors was allowed to decrease until it fell into single figures. At this stage the Privy Council had become a tight-knit group of virtually full-time, working politicians and administrators, very different from the unwieldy band of 40 that had served Mary, or even from Elizabeth's first council which had been half that size.

There was no definition of the Privy Council's powers or duties, but its members acted - and this seems to have been universally accepted - as if they were empowered to do whatever particular circumstances required. They issued proclamations in the queen's name which were generally taken as having the force of law. In economic affairs these frequently went as far as to amend existing legislation or even to anticipate acts of parliament that it was hoped would be passed in the future. Individuals were arrested and imprisoned at the council's command. Normally the 'crime' that had been committed was failing to carry out the council's instructions, and release could usually be obtained simply by promising to obey orders in future. At first sight it might seem surprising that the use of such powers did not cause a storm of protest among the political classes, whose members were increasingly aware of their rights. That they did not is both a warning against pre-dating the much celebrated Englishman's love of freedom, as some nineteenth-century historians tended to do, and an indication that councillors used their extensive powers sparingly and with wisdom. On most occasions wrongdoers seem to have been given the benefit of the doubt, and when action was taken the general opinion appears to have been that it was not before time. Certainly, there was never any feeling that the government was drifting towards tyranny or an abuse of power, and the few writers who have claimed that in the late sixteenth century England was on course to becoming a centralised autocracy have been guilty of stretching the evidence beyond reasonable bounds.

d) Regional Councils

In theory the Privy Council's powers were exercised in all parts of the queen's domains. In practice, however, action tended to be restricted to the English heartlands of the midlands, the south, East Anglia, and the south-west. Except when rebellion threatened or had already broken out, Ireland was left to the mercies of the royal representatives on the spot, and most of Wales was ignored (it was thought to be too distant and too inconsequential to merit more than passing attention). Two royally appointed regional councils dealt with the day-to-day administration of the outlying parts of England. The Council of the North, based in York (which was sometimes called the second capital of England despite the fact that monarchs almost never visited it), was responsible for most of the land to the north of the river Trent, while the Council of the Marches, based in Shropshire, looked after the districts on either side of the historic boundary between England and Wales. The perception of those in authority that the country was effectively London and the home counties writ large - a view that has given offence over many centuries to those who live at some distance from the capital - was already well established by the second half of the sixteenth century.

The machinery of central government was, of course, made up of more than the Exchequer, the law courts, and the Privy Council, but most of the other elements involved few people and had no great effect on the lives of the nation or the way in which it was governed. Typical of these was the Chancery - the department headed by the Lord Chancellor, who was also the Crown's leading law officer and the 'chairman' of the House of Lords - which was responsible for producing the official documents which gave legal form to royal grants and commands. It was staffed by a small number of clerks, most of whom appointed others to deputise for them, and who were staunch supporters of the time-honoured ways of working because these allowed them to make a comfortable living by extracting fees from those on whose behalf documents were drawn up. What was more significant were the departments that the central government did not contain. Besides the lack of provision for education and the social services (referred to at the start of the chapter), there was no proper machinery for dealing with the armed services, law and order, or foreign relations. As there was no regular army it was considered sufficient to make arrangements for the supply and control of troops as and when they were required. There was a standing navy but it was thought that this could be administered by one or two clerks. It is therefore hardly surprising that much of the money intended to be spent on armies and the navy was dissipated in inefficiency, waste and corruption. The maintenance of law and order was considered to be a matter to be dealt with by the localities, and it was only when disorder grew beyond the ability of local people to deal with that the government, in the form of the Privy Council, became involved. The Privy Council was also responsible for arranging those contacts with other states which the queen did not undertake herself through her dealings with their representatives when they attended on her. In 1572 a second post of Secretary was created and this allowed one person to devote the majority of his time to foreign affairs. However, there was still nothing approaching a co-ordinated approach to foreign policy: leading politicians with contacts abroad continued to plot and scheme, while the queen uneasily held the ring and, realising that she was starved of reliable evidence, normally decided that in the circumstances inaction was the least unsafe policy to adopt.

There was, of course, one other important element of the machinery of central government - parliament. But it will not be discussed here. Because it has been the focus of so much debate among historians a separate chapter has been devoted to it.

4 The Machinery of Local Government

In many countries 'local government' is the administration by the agents of the central government of the geographic units into which the state is divided. In England the tradition has been very different. Local government has been the control of localities by local people. During the past century this has been done by elected councils which have mostly been based on historic divisions such as parishes, boroughs and counties. In earlier centuries, and certainly during Elizabeth's reign, a district's 'natural' leaders were those in charge. In rural areas, where the vast majority of the population lived, this meant the major landowners (land was thought of as by far the most prestigious source of wealth), while in the towns and cities the richer traders were considered to be the leaders of their communities. Even if there had not been a systematic way of nominating those who were to wield power it is probable that the same people would have been in control, as leadership was expected of them, especially by their fellow property owners. It is significant that they also expected it of themselves.

a) Justices of the Peace (JPs)

Starting in the middle ages, and firmly established by the mid-sixteenth century, there was a system for identifying those who were to be responsible in the eyes of the law for what happened in the localities. Every year lists were prepared in Chancery showing the names of those who were to serve as justices on the commission of the peace (JPs) for each county. Although the lists were issued in the monarch's name, they were in fact drawn up by officials who had taken advice from the territorial magnates of each part of the country. The aim was to include all the most important landowners, but as the concept of 'most important' was never quantified, and as increasing numbers of men sought to have themselves included in this elite category, there was a tendency for the length of the list to grow year by year. It proved difficult to keep this trend within reasonable bounds, and it was only because of regular chivvying from the queen, allied to a hardening policy of excluding those of known Catholic sympathies from the lists, that much more than a hundred per cent increase in the number of JPs during the reign was avoided.

As far as is known, aspiring JPs did not offer cash inducements to those with the power to influence the composition of the commissions of the peace. Possibly this was because there was no financial gain to be made - either directly or indirectly - from being a JP. In fact, those selected were likely to be out of pocket as a result of carrying out the unpaid duties that went with the honour. For example, they were expected to travel to meetings that were normally held in the county town. The most important of these gatherings were the Quarter Sessions, which were held four times each year. Their main purpose was for magistrates (as JPs were called) to make collective decisions on the many issues for which legislation over the years had made them responsible. The most time-consuming of these, year in and year out, were the making of provision for the poor and the framing of regulations relating to wages and employment. In times of dearth the task of ensuring that sufficient supplies of food were available was also quite demanding. In addition to the routine tasks - including trying those criminal cases which were too serious to be dealt with by individual magistrates but which did not warrant referral to a Crown Court - Quarter Sessions were used to transact whatever specific items of business the Privy Council had written asking to be done. Very often this was a matter of gathering information to be forwarded to London. On a day-to-day basis JPs were expected to deal with whatever cases, especially of petty crime and of breaches of public order, were brought to their attention.

Historians have generally adopted a laudatory tone when writing about the work done by JPs in Elizabethan England. The impression has been given that the country was fortunate to be served by about 1800 unpaid volunteers who gave up significant amounts of their time in order to meet the needs of their communities. It has also been implied that the government was somewhat remiss in that it took advantage of the magistrates' goodwill by constantly adding to the burden of the duties JPs were required to perform. Almost habitually attention has been drawn to the fact that by the end of Elizabeth's reign JPs were expected to enforce over 300 statutes, a quarter of which had been added to the list since 1558. The 'striking fact' normally presented is that William Lambarde's *Eirenarcha,* which was essentially an instruction manual for JPs, had passed the 600 page mark by its 1599 edition.

Yet it may be that all this is somewhat misleading. It is probable that JPs as a body were neither as altruistic nor as hard working as has customarily been suggested. If one poses the question 'Why did the volunteers volunteer?', the most persuasive answers are likely to have to do with self-interest. On a conscious level the vast majority of JPs wished to be included on the commissions for the peace - and certainly not to be struck off in subsequent years once they had been included - because inclusion conferred on them considerable power and prestige within their community. As magistrates they were granted authority over their neighbours when they broke the law or fell upon hard times, and their status as being a cut above those of the local gentry who were not JPs received official confirmation. It is likely that further back in their consciousness they were motivated by the fear of civil commotion that seems to have been virtually universal among property owners during this period. It appears that the prevailing perception amongst the 'haves' was that society was perpetually on the edge of an abyss and in danger of toppling over into a state of lawlessness in which the 'have nots' (the majority of the population, who owned no property of value) would rise up and seize or destroy the possessions of their 'betters'. It was therefore very much in their interest to do whatever was necessary to ensure that the cataclysm they feared was warded off for as long as possible. There can be no doubt that many JPs thought of themselves as performing a public service by protecting civilisation as they knew it, but it is difficult for the historian judging with the benefit of hindsight to reach a more flattering conclusion than that, as a group, JPs were acting from a sense of enlightened self-interest.

Just as the portrayal of magistrates as selfless public servants is open to challenge, so the view of them as overworked and put-upon is of questionable validity. It is clear that had JPs diligently performed all that was required of them they would have been very active on the public's behalf, but it is very doubtful that this was the case. The evidence is only very partial, and in no sense could be claimed to be representative, but what is known suggests that the performance of most JPs was less than whole-hearted. It seems that Quarter Sessions were only a pale imitation of what they were expected to be. At each gathering only a few hours in total were spent discussing the wide range of issues that should have been kept under active consideration. In these circumstances it is likely that only a small amount of the monitoring that should have been done could have taken place. The small number of prosecutions brought under the legislation JPs were responsible for implementing suggests that this was so. In particular, magistrates seem to have been very lax in ensuring that those who failed to carry out their legal obligation to protect the interests of wage labourers and the poor were called to account. This impression of a less than rigorous approach to their responsibilities is reinforced by the evidence on attendance at Quarter Sessions. The large majority of JPs appear to have been conspicuous by their absence, and it has been estimated that between 80 and 90 per cent of them were routinely unable to be present. This must have meant that meetings were of a manageable size but it does not add substance to any contention that JPs were devoted public servants. It seems that considerable numbers of magistrates were more interested in acquiring the status of the position than in carrying out the duties that accompanied it.

b) Sheriffs

During the middle ages it was customary for the king to appoint one of his followers in each county to act as his representative, ensuring that two-way communication was maintained between the court and the localities. In particular, this official, the sheriff, was responsible for making certain that the king's orders, in the form of writs, reached their correct destinations and were acted on. By the sixteenth century being asked to act as sheriff was thought to be a dubious honour. While it was taken to be a sign of recognition of high social standing, it was resented as bringing with it a large number of time-consuming and unavoidable duties which were bound to leave the post holder considerably out of pocket. The custom that had become established by Elizabeth's reign reflected this ambivalent attitude. Most leading members of the gentry were prepared to serve as sheriff provided it was only for one year and provided that they were only invited to accept the 'honour' once during their lifetime. Part of the customary arrangement was that not all counties need have a sheriff. This situation was made possible by what sheriffs there were being responsible for neighbouring counties which did not have sheriffs of their own. It is a clear sign of the basic unpopularity of this element in the system of local government among those who might be called upon to serve that when the Privy Council attempted to introduce legislation stipulating that there should be a sheriff for each county the move was resisted by the House of Commons. Clearly there was no possibility of the role of the sheriff being expanded to meet any new needs that arose.

c) Lords Lieutenant

During Edward VI's reign, when there was considerable civil unrest and when it was feared that there would be even more, it was thought to be a wise precaution to appoint somebody to each of the potential trouble spots who would be able to act in the king's name and to take speedy action whenever the need arose. The person chosen to fill the new position of Lord Lieutenant in each of the counties affected was the one who best fitted the twin criteria of being totally trusted by the central government and having considerable local influence as a major regional landowner. Over the succeeding generation the government found it so convenient to have Lords Lieutenant that what had started as a temporary expedient restricted to part of the country was extended to cover the whole of England and Wales on a permanent basis. By 1585 it was accepted that every county would have a Lord Lieutenant (although it was common for the same person to serve for several counties) and that Lords Lieutenant would be selected on the same basis as they had been from the beginning. In counties where there was no predominant landowner, or where the one there was, was not considered by the government to be unquestionably reliable, a member of the Privy Council was used to fill the role.

Because most Lords Lieutenant were either prominent courtiers or Privy Councillors, or both, they spent much of the year out of their counties. This meant that they very much acted as figureheads who appeared in their official capacity only rarely, although they were always on hand should the situation appear particularly threatening. Most of their nominal duties were carried out by their deputies. In most counties there were a few (up to six in larger counties) of these. They were chosen from the upper ranks of the resident gentry and they appear to have been quite content to serve - to deputise for a peer was socially desirable, and the work they were called upon to do seems to have been regarded as of high status, in contrast to that of the sheriff. Deputy Lords Lieutenant were usually responsible for conducting the annual county muster in which all men fit and affluent enough to bear arms gathered together to practise some of the manoeuvres they would need to perform should they be required to put down an insurrection or ward off an invasion. During the second half of Elizabeth's reign the amateur leadership of the counties' military endeavours was assisted by professional Muster Masters. These full-time soldiers soon became highly unpopular. This was both because of what they did - for example, they were empowered to demand assistance with the movement and storage of arms and military supplies - and for the way in which they did it - they tended not to act with the deference that their social superiors expected. In addition, they were somewhat unfairly blamed for making it necessary to raise a county rate (a tax paid by landowners) to pay their wages and to purchase the goods that were required to keep the county militia in a state of operational readiness.

It has sometimes been suggested that the system headed by the Lords Lieutenant is a good example of the effective co-operation between central and local government that has been said to typify the healthy state of late-Tudor politics - referred to flatteringly as the 'Elizabethan balance'. For instance, attention has been drawn to the fact that about 100,000 men in total were recruited for military service abroad by means of this system. However, it seems likely that the praise has been somewhat over-lavish. While it has to be admitted that the country's military preparedness would have been minimal without the work of the Lords Lieutenant and their teams, it is doubtful whether their endeavours made a significant qualitative difference. Of course, the county militias were never put to the test, but the anecdotal evidence that exists suggests that, whereas the men of the militia might have held their own against a disorganised rabble, they would have been found woefully inadequate if faced by even a small professional army. This is even allowing for the fact that their potential should not be judged according to the quality of the troops raised for service overseas. Most of these were drawn from the dregs of society. They were of unsound health, were completely untrained, and their motivation could hardly have been lower. It is no wonder that their performance was catastrophic, even by the least demanding standards of the time. Perhaps the most telling fact relating to the quality of the militia is that, during the one crisis in which it seemed probable that the country would face invasion (in 1588), the queen chose to entrust her personal safety to the armed retinues of her leading peers rather than to the men trained via the county musters.

d) Was Local Government 'Local'?

Historians have quite rightly questioned how far local government in Elizabethan England was 'local' as opposed to controlled from the centre. The suspicion has existed that, although the role of JPs (who were local worthies rather than official from the centre) was crucial to the working of the local government system, the localities were in fact tightly controlled from London. There is much to be said in favour of this argument. While it is true that most JPs were independent-minded local gentry, there is no doubt that the body of magistrates, as a whole, was very susceptible to pressure from central government. They must have been painfully aware that the system of annual appointments to the commissions of the peace meant that they could not afford to give the least offence to those with influence at court. The non-reappointment of numerous individuals and, progressively, of Catholics as a group proved that their perception was correct. But not only the composition of the magistrates' benches was controlled from the centre: many of their activities were also prescribed for them. In normal times a county's JPs were collectively sent letters from the Privy Council detailing a number of tasks that should be undertaken, and when local conditions were harsh or unstable the flow of letters from the council to JPs, individually as well as collectively, tended to become a flood. And there is sound evidence that, when the focus of conciliar attention was on a locality, compliance by JPs to instructions received was speedy and complete. This picture of the counties being very much under the influence of the centre becomes even clearer when the situation in England is compared with that in two other countries, France and Spain, which were at a comparable stage of political development. In both Valois France and Habsburg Spain the central governments struggled in vain to exercise the degree of control over the localities that was commonplace in Tudor England. However, care must be taken not to overestimate the ability of Elizabethan government to impose its wishes anywhere. Considerable as it was compared to what was happening elsewhere in the sixteenth-century world, it fell far short of the system in France a century later when the powers of the *intendants* were at their height, and it was not a patch on what has been possible in modern times. The Privy Council's 23 messengers could not hope to rival a national postal service, let alone a telephone system or a set of networked computers.

5 The Chronology of Elizabethan Politics

Those who have studied any part of the political history of Britain during the past two centuries will be used to establishing a chronological framework in terms of changes in government. The key facts would be the names of the party in power and the prime minister. In dealing with Elizabethan England this system of establishing political landmarks does not apply. Governments did not change, there were no political parties in the modern sense, and the idea of a prime minister leading a team of followers to form an administration had not yet been thought of.

Throughout the period 1558-1603 the government of England was Queen Elizabeth. She was assisted by her Privy Council, the ancient departments of state (especially the Exchequer and Chancery), and the law courts. Those members of the Privy Council who carried out most administration and who advised her most frequently are often described as her ministers, although the term is one of convenience. It had no official standing. The queen took advice when and from whom she desired. Sometimes the opinion of the Privy Council as a body was requested, sometimes particular councillors (but not others) were consulted, and sometimes the views of courtiers who were not councillors were solicited. Elizabeth always thought about the advice she was given - often for a very long time, to the frustration of those who were in a hurry to get things done - before deciding what action, if any should be taken.

Although there was an underlying continuity to the political system throughout Elizabeth's reign, historians have managed to highlight one main aspect of change in order to establish a chronological framework for politics. The area of political life that has been chosen is the rivalry been the major players of politics at court. This has proved to be a manageable analytical tool both because the relative influence of the men involved ebbed and flowed over the years, and because it has sometimes been possible to identify policy differences between them.

However, it should be remembered that by drawing attention to changes and differences historians have, almost certainly unintentionally, exaggerated the disagreements that existed. What bound the politicians together (especially a strong commitment to the continued existence of the Elizabethan régime) was always much more important than what divided them (notably personal rivalry and disagreements over foreign policy).

With minor variations, most historians have been in agreement about identifying four 'periods' in the politics of Elizabeth's reign. However, it would generally be accepted that the price to be paid for establishing such a neat pattern has been considerable oversimplification and the ignoring of some facts that do not fit in with it. Nevertheless, the resulting framework is useful when attempting to bring intellectual order to an apparently chaotic situation, as long as it is remembered that the result is only a very rough approximation to reality.

a) The Early Years

The first few years of the reign seem to possess a political unity. This was the time when the régime was being established. Sir William Cecil enjoyed unrivalled political prominence. He was what could be meaningfully described as Elizabeth's chief minister, in that she paid much more attention to his advice than to that of others, and in that he was responsible for co-ordinating the implementation of most policy decisions at home and abroad. At times he worried desperately that he was about to loose his preeminent position - especially in late 1560 when it seemed likely that the queen would marry Lord Robert Dudley (see page 102) - but his fears always proved to be exaggerated. He remained the most politically influential man in the realm.

By stages between 1562 and 1565 the first period of Elizabethan politics came to an end. Cecil lost his position of unchallenged supremacy as others were allowed to vie with him in matters of both policy and patronage. The first addition to the ranks of those who wielded major political influence was Lord Robert Dudley, who joined the Privy Council in 1562 and was created Earl of Leicester in 1564 - he will be referred to as Leicester henceforth in this account. His political ambitions (like his self-confidence) knew no bounds, and he quickly established for himself the reputation of being prepared to go to whatever lengths were necessary, regardless of principle, to achieve his objectives. A third focal point for political influence was established in 1565 when the Earl of Sussex returned from service in Ireland and became a Privy Councillor. Sussex was one of the few able members of the 'old' aristocracy (those who could trace their titles and their ancestry well back into the middle ages) left in England. He was a traditionalist in all matters, especially religion, and he drew to him most of those who yearned for a return to times past. The foremost of his close associates was the Duke of Norfolk, England's premier peer and possessor of the only dukedom that had survived into the Elizabethan age. Norfolk's huge social prestige was matched by his monumental political incompetence and a lack of resolution which bordered on cowardice.

b) Faction Fighting

The three-cornered rivalry involving Cecil, Leicester and Sussex dominated the second period of Elizabethan politics. It lasted until 1572. It was typified by virulent faction-fighting at court, with plot being followed by counter-plot, and the tactics of deceit and treachery becoming the common currency of day-to-day politics. Leicester, in particular, showed himself to be lacking in all scruples. While Sussex acted (as he saw it) with honour in his constant championing of the 'conservative' cause, and Cecil wrapped up the pursuit of self-interest within a genuine commitment to the queen's interests and the maintenance of the Protestant Settlement - he used 'dirty tricks', but nearly always in retaliation - Leicester veered from extreme Protestant views to allying himself with the Catholic cause as seemed best to suit his short-term needs.

The destructiveness of much of the politics of the later-1560s, when Leicester was reckless in his determination to annihilate Cecil, gave rise to the one occasion when the Elizabethan régime was seriously threatened. Two distinct strands of potential opposition to the *status quo* came together in 1569. A plot was hatched at court by the Sussex and the Leicester factions whereby the Duke of Norfolk would marry Mary, Queen of Scots, who was a fugitive in England (see page 108 for a fuller explanation), and Elizabeth would be coerced into nominating any children of the match as her successors were she not to have children of her own. Part of the arrangement was to be the elimination of Cecil as a political force. He would be replaced by pro-Catholic sympathisers - Mary, Queen of Scots was a Catholic, as was Norfolk in all but name - and the traditional policy of friendship with the Habsburgs (in the form of Philip II of Spain) would be renewed. The second strand of the conspiracy was provided by the Catholic Earls of Northumberland and Westmorland who were the largest landowners in the counties immediately south of the Scottish border. Until the advent of the Tudors their ancestors had been quasi-independent rulers of their territories, but in recent generations a concerted attempt had been made by those in control in London to limit their powers dramatically. Under Elizabeth, for example, neither earl was appointed to a position of authority either in his own locality or nationally. Both men correctly concluded that they were being presented with a stark choice: they could either claim their rightful status by exerting force or they could remain quiet and see their position continue to be eroded. They were of a mind to select the former option and the Norfolk plot seemed to offer them their opportunity. It was agreed that they and their followers would march south to ensure that Elizabeth would have no choice but to accept the demands of the plotters at court.

Fortunately for Cecil the plans of the plotters were too complex and involved too many people to stand much chance of remaining secret. Once the queen was told the outline of what was intended the conspirators' hope of achieving success by the threat of force, rather than by its actual use, disappeared. What many had persuaded themselves would be no more than political manoeuvring would now have to be open rebellion or nothing. The London-based plotters immediately ran for cover, leaving Norfolk to face the queen's anger in a state of abject servility. The Northern Earls, shamed it is said by the jibes of the Countess of Westmorland, decided that they were too far implicated to be able to back down in safety. They therefore assembled their men, marched to Durham, reinstated the Mass in the cathedral, and called upon the country to rise up to restore the true faith. Their appeal went largely unheeded and, with their own men melting away and an army loyal to the queen approaching, they could do little but flee to what they mistakenly believed would be the safety of Scotland. But the fact that the Revolt of the Northern Earls of 1569 ended so tamely should not blind us to the danger that the situation represented. Had all those involved in the scheme acted with determination there is every possibility that success would have been theirs. Certainly Elizabeth would have had the greatest difficulty in raising troops had it appeared that hers might be the losing side. Those historians who have claimed that the Elizabethan régime came close to destruction in 1569 will, of course, never be able to prove their case, but they have marshalled an impressive amount of circumstantial evidence to support their argument.

Once Norfolk had capitulated unreservedly and Elizabeth had chosen to accept Leicester's protestations of innocence the crisis was over. So was the threat to Cecil's position. Although it was not until 1572 that the forces of Protestantism prevailed upon the queen to authorise Norfolk's execution, the conservatives had become a discredited political force by the time the Northern Revolt was over. At the same time, Leicester seems to have been chastened by his lucky escape and to have decided that he must learn to live with Cecil - if not in harmony, at least within the bounds of 'normal' political activity. Thus the second and very volatile period of Elizabethan political history came to an end. The scene was set for the long period of mid-Elizabethan stability.

c) Mid-Elizabethan Stability

Although all was not sweetness and light between the competing politicians during the 1570s and 1580s, the emphasis was very much on co-operation between them so that the existing régime would be safeguarded. The two men of major influence were Burghley (as Cecil became in 1571) and Leicester. Both were leaders of large factions made up of followers who hoped to obtain position or financial gain from their adherence to their patron's cause. Men joined whichever faction seemed to offer them the best prospects of advancement. Family background seems to have been the major determinant influencing the choice made. Matters of principle or issues of policy preference appear to have been significant for only a small number of people. Those who were affected in this way were almost all Protestants who took their religion very seriously (often lumped together somewhat misleadingly as Puritans). They tended to gravitate towards Leicester who, after his potentially disastrous flirting with the Catholic camp in the late-1560s, rapidly established himself as the leader of those who wished to make England the champion of the Protestant cause throughout Europe. Even when faction-fighting was at its height in the 1560s it had been possible for people of ambition to stand apart from the main groupings as long as they had sufficient social standing or an independent route to the queen's ear. In the 1570s and 1580s the number of 'independent' politicians grew considerably, especially if one includes those whose attachment to either the Burghley or the Leicester factions was so loose that it was not of great significance.

It is customary to speak of the 'big four' when describing the politics of the mid-Elizabethan period. Besides Burghley and Leicester the major figures were Sir Christopher Hatton and Sir Francis Walsingham. Hatton was a courtier-turned-politician. He rose from obscurity - he was the younger son of a country gentleman - on the strength of his charm and personality which, allied to his good sense and sound (but not outstanding) ability, allowed him to win and to retain the queen's special favour. He seems to have been genuinely devoted to her, a fact that Elizabeth clearly recognised. She valued his opinion very highly, presumably because she was confident that it would be shaped neither by self-interest nor by commitments to anybody but herself. Hatton was the man who came closer than anyone else to fitting the conventional image of the 'faithful retainer'. Walsingham was very different. He was first and foremost a professional politician. From 1573 to 1590 he was one of the queen's two Principle Secretaries - the post was split into two soon after Burghley relinquished it following his elevation to the peerage - and he was powerfully driven by his strong commitment to radical Protestantism. In most situations he sided with Leicester when the leading two of the 'big four' had a difference of opinion, but he retained sufficient independence to be 'his own man'. Much of his influence resulted from the fact that it was he who very often decided what information should (and should not) reach the queen.

There is no reason to believe that the consensus politics that gave rise to the much vaunted 'Elizabethan stability' would have ended had the big four remained active. As it was, a virtual 'clean sweep' occurred within the space of four years. Leicester died in 1588. He was followed by Walsingham in 1590 and Hatton in 1591. Although Burghley survived until 1598, from 1592 he was a sick man who spent much of his time in bed. During these years of poor health he was only an irregular participant in the affairs of state. All this meant that political leadership passed into other hands, thus bringing to an end the third of the periods into which Elizabethan political life may conveniently be divided.

d) The Nineties

It was the fourth of the reign's periods - normally referred to as 'the nineties' - that has caused the most controversy among historians. It used generally to be agreed that the last decade of Elizabeth's life was one during which the régime began to crumble. It was even suggested that had the queen lived a few years longer politics would have become so divisive that prolonged civil strife might have resulted, with the civil war that eventually broke out in 1642 taking place a generation earlier. Since about 1980 a number of revisionist historians have argued that the orthodox interpretation has greatly exaggerated the extent to which the 1590s witnessed a slide towards the breakdown of governmental authority. But not everybody has been convinced by the case advanced by the revisionists. Some writers maintain that there was a danger of the pendulum swinging too far. Such has been the significance accorded to the nineties in recent historical debate that the issues involved will be discussed in a separate chapter.

The aim of this section has been to establish a simple chronological framework within which Elizabethan politics can be understood. In the process, the part played by the queen in political life has been almost completely ignored. This vital dimension of English political history between 1558 and 1603 provides the thread that runs through the remainder of the book.

Making notes on Government and Politics

The mass of information included in this chapter might best be described as 'background' in that it is made up of information and ideas you will need to understand in order to make sense of the rest of the book. You are unlikely ever to need to reproduce it directly in an examination. You therefore need to make the briefest (if any) notes on it. Possibly the most effective notes will result from using the section titles as your headings and restricting yourself to just one sentence of notes per section.

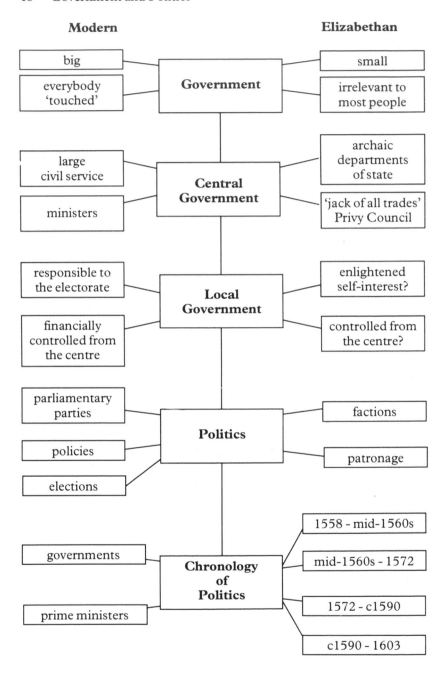

Summary - Government and Politics

CHAPTER 4

Elizabeth and her Servants

1 Introduction

From the highest to the lowest in the land people were proud in Elizabethan England to be described as the queen's servant. It was decidedly an honour to serve the monarch, and it was one that was much sought after. Such had long been the normal state of affairs in England and throughout most of Western Europe. Sometimes the links in the master-servant chain were weakened when a ruler acted in a way that made him appear unworthy to be served, but even then the idea that one was serving an institution rather than the temporary holder of the position was often sufficient to overcome the sense of dishonour that carrying out the wishes of a disreputable monarch brought with it. When it was not, rebellion normally ensued. This could be the prelude to a prolonged period of civil war, as it had been in the second half of the fifteenth century once Henry VI's shortcomings had been found to be unendurable by a majority of the nobility.

There was no danger that Elizabeth I would be found to be a monarch unworthy to be served. She avoided the three major pitfalls that had led some of her predecessors into difficulties. On occasions English kings had failed to project a sufficiently 'grand' image to confer prestige on those who served them. Although Elizabeth tended to be careful with money to the point of meanness, she recognised that expenditure on the minor trappings of monarchy, especially fine clothes and jewellery, was an essential element in the process of establishing and maintaining her status as a fitting ruler. She was resolute in her refusal to be tempted to spend large sums of money on building new palaces or on upgrading those she already possessed, but she was insistent that no expense be spared in ensuring she was constantly surrounded by that pomp and ceremony which would both impress all those who saw it and dignify those who played subordinate roles to her in the proceedings. The writings of foreign visitors who witnessed the queen 'in action' indicate that the intended effect was generally created.

The downfall of several English kings had been precipitated by their inability or unwillingness to accord appropriate precedence, influence and status to the elite of major landowners who were collectively known as the magnates, the barons or the peers. Instead of nurturing the support of this small group of men (there were rarely as many as 50 of them at any time), the unsuccessful kings tended to surround themselves with favourites from outside this circle whom they often attempted to elevate as high or higher than 'established' families by awarding them titles which carried with them considerable status and precedence according to the complex set of rules governing such matters. This blatant and even pointed disregard of the social *status quo* caused great resentment. This was sometimes sufficient in itself to trigger off a rebellion. It could be argued that Elizabeth came near to committing errors of this kind by extending her favour to numerous 'new' men (most notably Sir William Cecil and Lord Robert Dudley) and by ignoring the Northern magnates (especially the Earls of Northumberland and Westmorland), thereby inciting them to open rebellion (see page 45). However, such a verdict would be very unbalanced. In nearly all situations the queen exhibited great awareness and considerable sensitivity over even minor issues affecting the honour and status of her leading subjects. She was always quick to insist that precedence be given to members of the nobility according to the rank and antiquity of their titles, although this meant that her special favourites had to give way to those whom they might have thought themselves superior to because of the special affection Elizabeth felt towards them. She protected the high status associated with a title of nobility by being ultra cautious in granting new ones. She even claimed that the criteria used for judging the guilt of members of the highest ranks in society should be more generous than for their inferiors. When she was presented with evidence that the Duke of Norfolk, the premier peer of the realm, had played a part in a conspiracy against her, she was very reluctant to allow him to be tried. When he was found guilty and was condemned to death, she only agreed to his execution when a high degree of political pressure was applied to her. Over a long period those interested in such matters were left in no doubt that the queen was as concerned about maintaining the privileges of rank as were the most prickly of her subjects.

Some English kings had provoked violent opposition by falling under the political influence of their circle of friends, to the detriment of those whose rank and position led them to expect that their advice would be taken seriously. Elizabeth developed a complex series of inter-connected strategies in order to avoid this potential pitfall. First and foremost she took great care to demonstrate that she was very much her own woman and that she was under the regular influence of no individual or group. There is even the suspicion that she sometimes refused to follow what she regarded as being well-founded suggestions because it was known that she had recently accepted advice from the same quarter on several occasions and she did not wish it to be thought that she was making a habit of doing so! She actively maintained her right to seek advice wherever she wished, refusing to be restrained by either convention (for example, that the Privy Council should routinely be consulted on all matters of political significance) or rules of her own making (for example, that she did not listen to the opinions of members of her household on matters of public interest). This allowed her from time to time to massage the egos of those substantial landowners who were not a part of the court circle by taking special steps to elicit their advice on issues she thought were particularly important to them.

A third of her strategies was to insist that those who had contact with her operated in watertight compartments. Thus those who waited on her on a daily basis were discouraged from using their proximity to their sovereign to advance any political cause or to influence the distribution of patronage. The fact that a shrewd lady-in-waiting or a cunning gentleman usher could ensure that selected tit-bits of information came to Elizabeth's attention, and that members of the household were frequently approached by courtiers either to report on or to influence the queen's mood should not be allowed to obscure the great success in general terms that was achieved in eliminating the household as a forum of political activity. Elizabeth employed this technique as effectively as any British monarch during the period when kings and queens ruled as well as reigned, and much more successfully than most. Much the same approach - although it was implemented much less strictly - was adopted towards the social aspects of court life. Just because a courtier spent a lot of time in close social contact with Elizabeth did not mean that he thereby acquired political influence. Even those who achieved the status of favourites were sometimes denied any say in affairs of state. The Earl of Oxford and Sir Walter Ralegh were at different times very close to the queen's affections but they were not allowed to build political careers on the basis of the special relationship that they enjoyed. Two favourites - Lord Robert Dudley (Earl of Leicester) and Sir Christopher Hatton - did develop the twin roles of close friend of the queen and major political figure, but in each case this happened at Elizabeth's specific instigation. It was not a matter of close social contact being allowed to spill over into political influence. The queen was remarkably successful in keeping the two aspects of her life separate. Leicester and Hatton were prominent in political as well as social activity because Elizabeth made the conscious decision that they were well-fitted to shoulder governmental responsibility. In both cases the queen handled a favourite's transition from friend to prominent politician with skill and sensitivity. In fact, it has even been claimed that the way in which she handled the elevation of Leicester to major political responsibility was one of her outstanding achievements in statecraft. Elizabeth was almost always careful to ensure that anybody who was to have some regular political influence in central government was 'marked' as being in this position by being made a member of the Privy Council. Because the Privy Council was generally recognised as the forum in which discussions about matters of state normally took place, this method of proceeding removed any possibility of resentment being caused by fears that somebody was exercising secret, 'back-stairs' political influence.

The more active members of the Privy Council have been labelled 'ministers' by historians. It is these 'ministers', and the queen's dealings with them, that have created most interest among historians. Two in particular - William Cecil (Lord Burghley) and Lord Robert Dudley (Earl of Leicester) - have been the subjects of major attention. The issues that have been explored most frequently have been the way in which the two men 'operated' and the interaction between them and the queen. These concerns will provide the structure for the consideration of the two most important of Elizabeth's servants which follows.

2 Sir William Cecil, Lord Burghley

a) Background

William Cecil was a member of the third generation of a minor court family which had 'emerged' from the obscurity of the border lands of England and Wales as followers of Henry VII when he seized power in 1485. William's grandfather and father had acquired sufficient land in south-west Lincolnshire and north-east Northamptonshire to win for themselves a place among the leading gentry of the district. They also consolidated the family's status as loyal, if relatively unimportant, servants of the Crown. William, who was born in 1520, grew up surrounded by the expectation that he would continue the family tradition. His education was geared to this end. After a grammar school education which provided him with a sound grounding in Latin, he was sent to Cambridge University for his intellectual skills to be developed as extensively as possible. From there he proceeded to the Inns of Court in London. There he received a training in common law, the legal system operated in most of the king's law courts. Cecil was the first member of his family to undergo this experience which had recently become accepted as vital for all those who wished to play any part in public life as well as for those who intended to follow a career in the legal profession.

Once Cecil had completed his formal education his father ensured that an opening was made available to him in the lower ranks of the machinery of central government. In a system which normally rewarded social rank (who you were) and influence (who you knew) rather than ability (what you could do), Cecil was fortunate not to spend his whole life functioning at the low level for which his birth was thought to fit him. His good fortune was to be at court during the uncertain years of the reign of Edward VI (1547-53) when 'new' men were in the ascendancy. These were prepared to favour other 'new' men provided they had something special to offer. There was no doubt that Cecil fell into this category. His combination of very sound intellectual ability, administrative competence, and proven reliability marked him out as one of the most promising younger men in government service. Although he was judged to be dependable and loyal, he was also thought of as a man of independence. Therefore he was able to survive the disgrace of one patron (the Duke of Somerset) and to transfer his allegiance to the new man in power (the Duke of Northumberland) without creating ill-feeling or suspicion. In 1550 his talents were fully recognised when he was appointed the second (and definitely junior) of the king's secretaries. He acquitted himself well (he was efficient, showed sound judgement, and was suitably self-effacing) and seemed to have a distinguished administrative career ahead of him. But all that changed when Edward died in 1553. There was no possibility that the Catholic Mary would wish to make use of the services of the avowedly Protestant Secretary. The most that Cecil could hope for was that he would be permitted to retire to his estates in peace. It says much for his reputation as a man of honour that this is what he was allowed to do once he had given his word that he would do nothing to oppose the new regime.

For five years the ex-Secretary primarily devoted himself to building up his family's property and influence in its home area. The contact he retained with the world of national politics was tenuous. From time to time he carried out minor representative duties for the queen and was even elected as an MP on one occasion, but most significantly he continued to serve Princess Elizabeth as the person overseeing her estates. This meant that he maintained a minimal contact with her. However, this link was not sufficiently strong for it ever to be suspected that he was party to any of the plots that were thought to exist to replace Mary with her Protestant sister. Nevertheless, Elizabeth had clearly formed a very positive impression of Cecil. When she became queen one of her first actions was to ask him to become her Principal (and only) Secretary. Cecil was very pleased to accept the invitation. Thus began a close working relationship that was to last for 40 years, until it was ended by the minister's death in 1598. It was the longest such partnership in British history.

b) The Man

William Cecil (he was knighted in 1551 and created Lord Burghley in 1571) was much more consistent than most men in the public eye, both in his own and other times. However, he was not entirely so. As a result there are exceptions to almost every generalisation that can be made about him. But they were exceptions that proved the rule. And, of course, they were exceptions that made him all the more human. Certainly he was not the automaton that some writers have portrayed him as being.

Cecil's family background had a major effect on the way he acted throughout his life. Both his father and his grandfather had made a conscious policy of limiting their ambition because they believed that those who overreached themselves were likely to attract the envy of their peers and the hostility of their betters, which might result in all being lost. They adopted a safety-first strategy of satisfying themselves with small gains and, in the words of one commentator, 'studying not to give offence'. Their top priority was to ensure that they made no enemies, even if by doing so they had to give up some opportunities to enrich themselves. William's initial inclination in all situations was to act in the same way. There were times, especially in the 1590s (see page 129), when he risked alienating others by battling in his own interest, but there were many more occasions on which he backed down rather than risk being thought to be overstepping the mark. The most striking example of this type of behaviour was when, late in his life, he declined the queen's offer to promote him to an earldom. It seems that this remarkable decision was made partly because he (correctly) believed that the raising of the son of a minor official to such an exalted rank would cause offence among those whose families had held senior peerages for generations. He would rather be thought of as a man who

Lord Burghley riding his mule in his garden

knew his place than as a man who had allowed himself to be over-promoted. It might be thought that because he died a very rich man he had turned his back on the family tradition of exercising caution in the pursuit of self-interest. But this is not so. When the surviving records are examined two facts stand out most clearly: that Cecil ignored many opportunities to enrich himself during his 45 years of government service in senior positions, and that the wealth he did 'extract' was never money that others could realistically expect to be theirs. It would have been impossible for Cecil to acquire so much property without attracting envy, especially from those who were not in a position to do likewise, but it seems he was successful in ensuring that few people felt they had been denied financial gain by him.

The other family tradition that William adopted wholeheartedly was that the Cecils were first and foremost servants of the Crown. This meant that his loyalty to the Tudors was unquestioning and that there was no possibility that he would ever act in what he regarded as being a treacherous manner. Both Mary and Elizabeth recognised this and their belief in his trustworthiness was unshakable. This turned out to be an invaluable asset, especially on one or two occasions during Elizabeth's reign when his enemies worked hard to convince the queen that he was conspiring against her. They found it impossible to destroy the minister's credibility with the monarch even when it could be shown that he was acting against her express wishes in the mistaken belief that he knew better than she did what was in the Crown's best interest. At such times Elizabeth found it necessary to make public her displeasure at the way in which he had acted but there was never any doubt that he would be restored to her favour after an appropriate lapse of time. Cecil's desire to serve his queen was probably the single most important motivating force in his adult life. He has been quoted as saying, 'Serve God by serving the queen, for all other service is indeed bondage to the devil'.

William Cecil's education was a second major force in shaping the way in which he acted. His six years of study at Cambridge established patterns of thought and methods of problem-solving that were very apparent in the conduct of his official duties. His papers show that he was an inveterate list maker, especially when there was a policy decision on which he was called to advise. The neat columns of pros and cons appeared time and time again. He methodically assigned each of the relevant factors to one side or other of the argument, and drew up balanced conclusions once the listing was complete. The effect of training he received at the Inns of Court was also apparent in the way he perceived most problems. If his Cambridge experiences made him methodical and thorough, the Inns of Court were responsible for him being legalistic. His analyses of situations were therefore always very 'correct' but they appear cold and lacking in an appreciation of the human factors that were involved. One of the lessons that Cecil drew from the entirety of his education was that hard work is a virtue. As a result he became what nowadays would be described as a workaholic, allowing the seemingly endless flow of papers with which he had to deal to fill almost all his waking hours. What is more, he seems to have contentedly accepted that this was to be his lot in life.

When Cecil was at Cambridge it was a hotbed of Protestantism. The new beliefs were discussed at length by students and teachers alike, and most of those involved accepted them to a greater or lesser extent. Cecil was no exception. By the time he moved to London he was firmly convinced that the Bible contained the most accurate account of what God wished Christians to believe and that the teachings of the Catholic Church were mistaken in some key areas. But his 'conversion' was of the head rather than of the heart. There was no passion about his religious beliefs, although they were sincerely held. He was therefore content to abide by the arrangements that existed in Henry VIII's final years by which the authority of the Church of Rome was rejected while many of its teachings and practices were retained. He was also prepared to accept the more radical Protestant teachings and practices that were adopted during Edward VI's reign, but he did so with little enthusiasm. However, this does not mean that he was a lukewarm Protestant - he retained his commitment to his faith during Mary's reign, although he was prepared to conform to Catholic practices as the law directed him to do - but merely that he was a conservative one. He found the religious settlement of 1559 much to his liking, and subsequently saw no reason for it to be changed. Therefore he found himself out of sympathy both with the Puritans who wanted further major changes in the Church and with those at court, such as Leicester and Walsingham, who supported their cause during most of the 1570s and 1580s. This has led some historians to suggest that Cecil was a *politique,* someone who changed his religious beliefs to suit political convenience. This is understandable because there is an amount of evidence that seems to support this interpretation. However, it is much more convincing to argue that his moderate Protestant views were sincerely held and that it was sheer good fortune that they were politically expedient, especially in that they were a near-perfect match with those of Queen Elizabeth.

It seems that Cecil believed in moderation almost as a matter of principle. He certainly disliked extremism in whatever form it occurred. He was averse to seeing things as black or white: he was more at home with making judgements in terms of shades of grey. This made it possible for him to be very flexible in his approach to many issues, although it did lay him open to the charge that his main guiding light was expediency. And there is no doubt that he did occasionally shift his ground on moral issues because it was convenient to do so. However, he was generally consistent in his judgement of what was acceptable and what was not. For example, he was prepared to accept gifts of modest proportions from satisfied parties in cases he had tried - these he judged to be signs of reasonable gratitude - but he returned all gifts proffered before a case was decided or large gifts made once the outcome was known because he regarded the acceptance of such rewards as corruption. He seems to have had a very clear idea about where the dividing line between acceptable and unacceptable behaviour should be drawn, but it is not surprising that some historians, failing to find hard and fast lines, have suggested that the image of morality he liked to project was little more than a sham. Judged by the standards of today he was certainly open to criticism, but it might be thought more valid to judge his behaviour according to the standards of his time. Using that criterion he was certainly one of the most upright public figures of his age.

c) Administrator, Politician, and Statesman

In the sixteenth century the modern distinction between politicians and civil servants did not exist at the highest levels of central government. Those who served the monarch in a senior capacity were called upon to fulfil both roles. Nevertheless, for each person the balance between the two activities tended to differ. Thus there were those who were primarily administrators for whom politics was an unwelcome chore made necessary to protect their positions, and there were those who were politicians first and foremost but who were called upon to carry out administrative duties as members of the Privy Council. Cecil was one of the very rare people who became a leading light in both administration and the world of politics. In Elizabethan England he was unique in the extent to which this happened, although Sir Francis Walsingham also straddled both fields. However, he never approached Cecil's eminence as a politician.

i) Administrator

Cecil's background was in administration and he could have restricted himself largely to that area of activity had he so desired. The post of Secretary (often referred to as Principal Secretary) which he occupied from 1558 to 1572 was sometimes filled by a person who wished to be involved in politics as little as possible. Cecil's successor, Sir Thomas Smith, was such a person. But Cecil, encouraged by the queen, chose otherwise. He decided to use the enormous scope of his post to play as large a part as possible in formulating policy, and thus he became deeply involved in the morass of politics. But this was not done at the expense of his administrative duties which he carried out with great diligence, as far as his health would permit (he suffered from periodic bouts of depression and from gout which frequently flared up very painfully, right up to the time of his death. As Secretary during the first third of Elizabeth's reign he shouldered the full burden of the government's non-routine administrative activity. Much of this related to foreign policy and the seemingly endless round of negotiations with the rulers of Scotland, France and Spain. At the same time there was a whole host of domestic issues to be dealt with. The most time-consuming of these were the management of parliament, the investigation of potential and actual threats to public order, and the making of arrangements to cope with the effects of natural disasters. For example, the opening weeks of a parliamentary session or an event such as the Revolt of the Northern Earls in 1569 generated enough work to fill all the hours from dawn to dusk. It is therefore hardly surprising that when Cecil relinquished the secretaryship after 14 years it was thought that he had probably given his all. Little was it imagined that he would carry a heavy administrative load for a further 26 years.

Part of this burden was a continuation of what had been done before. For more than a year, until Sir Francis Walsingham was appointed as a second Secretary, Cecil found it necessary to oversee the work of his successor. But a longer-term continuation was the work generated by the Court of Wards, of which Cecil had been the Master (the person in charge) since 1562. He still held the position at the time of his death in 1598. In many respects the way in which he carried out his duties at the Court of Wards, which was responsible for deciding what should happen to children (and their property) who had inherited large landed estates, was typical of his whole approach to public affairs. He made a conscious decision about what his priority was to be in determining what should happen to each ward. This in itself was unusual, as was the decision made. It might have been expected that he would follow the pattern established during Henry VII's reign of selling wardships at the highest price possible so that the maximum amount of money would come to the Crown. Or if he had been seeking the greatest benefit for himself he might have ensured that wardships were granted to those who offered him the greatest inducements. But he did neither of these things. His decision was that he would act so as to protect the interests of the existing aristocracy. In keeping with this policy he took care to place each child where he or she would receive an upbringing appropriate to his or her station. He also granted the control of their lands to somebody of a similar social standing - despite the fact that higher bids were often available from social inferiors - so that the wealth of the nobility would remain within the same class. One result of this approach was that the Crown's income from wardship declined in real terms, once inflation has been taken into account, during the period of his stewardship.

A similar way of working is apparent in his conduct as Lord Treasurer, a post that he held from 1572 until his death. He might have continued the practice of the latter years of his predecessor, the Marquess of Winchester, who during his prolonged old age had treated the position as little more than a sinecure which conferred some wealth and considerable political and social standing while demanding little work in return. But he decided otherwise. He exploited the post's potential to the full and became the active co-ordinator of the Crown's finances. He used his position to protect the financial interests of the landed class in general and of the peerage in particular. He kept parliamentary taxes as low as possible while turning a blind eye to the fact that the system of self-assessment that was used in their collection was shamelessly exploited by those who should have been paying the most. The greatest landowners, including himself, were allowed to go unchallenged when they declared their incomes to be as little as 1 per cent and no more than 10 per cent of what they were in reality. In addition, the custom of the Crown making interest-free loans to members of the peerage so that they could continue to enjoy the life style that was expected of them was considerably extended, as was the practice of making little effort to ensure that the loans were ever repaid. The result of this approach was that the Crown's income shrunk during a time when ideally it should have grown to take account of the costs of the warfare which seemed incessant during the latter part of the reign.

Cecil's attitude towards the queen's income did not lead to disaster because it was linked to a consistent drive to confine expenditure to a minimum. In this he was assisted by Elizabeth, who had a marked dislike of spending money. Both therefore tended to resist those who advocated an aggressive foreign policy, and even in time of war they were reluctant to agree to expenditure on anything but defensive measures, unless there was a realistic hope that offensive expeditions would pay for themselves. In the circumstances historians have considered it to be something of a triumph that when Elizabeth died her debts only amounted to about one year's income. However, Cecil has been criticised for failing to take a longer-term view in his financial régime. It is clear that he was content to put off the evil hour of reforming the system in order to provide the Crown with the increased income that it plainly required in the changed circumstances of the later-sixteenth century. He doubtlessly recognised that the radical changes that were required would prove unpopular and it seems that he was pleased to leave it to a successor to grasp this particular nettle. Whether this is judged to be cowardice or political wisdom depends on one's point of view.

Despite the criticisms that have been levelled at Cecil, there is general agreement that as an administrator he ranks among the outstanding practitioners of his century, fit to be mentioned in the same breath as the two great Thomases, Wolsey and Cromwell, of Henry VIII's reign. But there is no suggestion that as a politician he is to be regarded nearly so highly. Nevertheless, he had considerable political skills that allowed him to hold his own with the other leading lights of his age, even if he was not able to outshine them.

ii) Politician

It used to be thought that Elizabethan politics was largely about factions and the in-fighting that took place between them. Although such views have been modified in recent years following the findings of numbers of revisionist historians, the role played by Cecil has generally not needed to be reinterpreted. This has largely been because he never was regarded as being a major participant in the faction fighting despite the fact that some of its most vicious attacks were directed against him. Cecil was not the typical leader of a faction, in that he did not demand public displays of loyalty to him from his clients in the same way that some aristocratic faction leaders did. His following was much more loosely organised than were those of his 'competitors'. This was because few of his supporters were linked to him by the semi-feudal ties that arose from the traditional territorial control exercised by major landowners. Most of his clients attached themselves to him because of the influence he wielded by virtue of the posts he held and of his closeness to the queen. These supporters even included peers who were faction leaders in their own right. The most important and constant of these was the Earl of Sussex who possessed a proud ancestry which he thought of as second to none - hence some of the bitterest disputes of the 1560s (see page 44). The Duke of Norfolk was also a highly influential, although less dependable, supporter during the 1560s.

Cecil did not pride himself - as most other leaders of factions did - on either the size or the quality of his clientage. Its members certainly received more from their patron than he ever demanded of them because Cecil called in the favours he was owed very sparingly. Nor were his favours restricted to his 'own people'. On many occasions he intervened in a dispute or interceded with the queen in the interests of one of his rivals, especially if he thought this was necessary to save the face of another councillor who had perhaps promised more than he was able to deliver. This was one way in which his belief in moderation affected his behaviour as a politician. He was competitive, but only to an extent that he considered reasonable. He did not expect to get his way all the time, recognising that it was healthy for the body politic for successes to be shared around. He would have had little sympathy with the 'winner takes all' approach of present-day party politics. It was in this area of maintaining things on an even keel that Cecil's political skills were particularly evident, and it was greatly to his credit that he remained on good personal terms even with those who attacked him most savagely or whose treatment of him was least defensible.

Some would argue that politics is, by definition, a dirty business. It certainly was in Elizabethan England. It is true that assassination was not an accepted 'trick of the trade' as it was in contemporary France, but there was certainly a need for Cecil and his fellow politicians to watch their backs in a metaphoric sense. Because the queen was the final decision-maker on all matters of importance rival politicians were caught up in an endless merry-go-round of intrigue to ensure that the influence they had with her was either maintained or increased. The action required was both offensive and defensive. The balance between the two modes varied from time to time depending on the situation and the individual politician's outlook. Cecil was most often on the defensive, both because his influence was normally in the ascendant and because he was satisfied with the *status quo*. Therefore his energies were more often directed towards stopping things happening than to trying to bring about change. A good example of Cecil operating in defensive mode was his campaign to prevent the marriage of the queen and Lord Robert Dudley in 1559-60. Even before Amy Robsart (Dudley's wife) died (see page 102) he was spreading the rumour that Dudley was planning to murder her so that he would be free to marry Elizabeth, and once the 'accident' had occurred he took active steps to fuel the suspicion that Dudley was responsible for Amy's death. He also added the weight of his reputation to the story that Dudley had struck a bargain with Philip II that England would be returned to obedience to Rome if Spanish influence were successful in persuading Elizabeth to marry her favourite. There is every reason to believe that Cecil acted as he did in order to make Dudley's position as a suitor untenable, and that he knew that there was little substance in the allegations he was circulating. Another dramatic example of Cecil's defensive political skills came in 1569 when the Duke of Norfolk allied with the Earl of Leicester in a plot to destroy him. Only by exercising all his political skills and by calling in many of the favours he was owed was the attack repelled. However, Cecil was much less successful when he was on the offensive. In general terms he lacked the willingness (alternatively described as courage or foolhardiness, depending on the observer's set of values) to play for the highest stakes unless compelled by others to do so.

iii) Statesman

There are many different definitions of the concept of 'statesman', but they share a number of common components. They all at least imply that a statesman is morally superior to a politician, that he places the interests of the state he serves before his own and those of his supporters, and that he takes a long-term view of issues, rather than being primarily influenced by the needs of the moment. There is no doubt that Cecil met these criteria sufficiently well to be regarded as a statesman. In particular, it is certain that he was strongly committed to upholding what he understood to be the English state, by which he meant the territory of England and Wales, and its political, religious and social systems. He also possessed a moral stature that marked him out from most of those who played a major part in the political life of Elizabethan England. This, of course, is not to claim that he was a paragon of virtue - he was much less of a puritan in public life than he was in his private life - but he established a reputation for being essentially trustworthy and honest in the things that mattered, and the surviving evidence suggests that this was deserved. When public interest was in conflict with his private interest, he believed that he always put the good of the country before his own. There have been suggestions that at times he deluded himself over this, but the claim that he generally sacrificed self-interest if it conflicted with what he considered to be his duty to the queen seems to be soundly based.

Given that there can be little dispute over the fact that Cecil's performance in public office entitles him to be considered a statesman, the main task of the historian is to make an assessment of the extent and the quality of his statesmanship. Because the criteria used in making such an assessment can legitimately vary and because much of the evidence lends itself to differing interpretations there is plenty of room for honest disagreement on this issue. The aspect of Cecil's work over which there is always likely to be the liveliest debate is his long-term policy formation. It has been the received wisdom for many years that he lacked imagination and flare. He has been portrayed as an able and conscientious work-horse who did not possess the ability to inspire either himself or others. It has been suggested that because he was essentially a pessimist - hence perhaps his bouts of depression - he spent much of his time fearing and doing his best to avoid the worst, which meant that his approach to most issues was of the short-term, finger-in-the-dyke type. This interpretation is supported by the many policy documents which he wrote and which have survived. This body of evidence also suggests that, especially in complex situations involving dealings with foreign powers, the quality of his work was not high. It was invariably clearly analysed and presented but was rarely very persuasive - it lacked the intangible quality of 'feel' which is recognisable when it is present but which is difficult to define when it is not. It is possible to construct a reasoned argument to support the view that he was a statesman who lacked vision - the sort of person who made an excellent second-in-command but who was no leader - and who therefore must be judged to have been a statesman of limited quality, even if he was clearly the most able of the counsellors available to the queen.

However, it is possible to overdo the argument that Cecil was a man who lacked vision, especially if 'lack of vision' is taken to mean 'lack of sense of direction'. Cecil may not have been very good at imagining things as being very different to how they were (vision), but he had definite views about how best to conserve the current state of affairs. He is said to have advised the queen to 'gratify your nobility, and principal persons of the realm, to bind them fast to you'. This was undoubtedly very sound advice on how to maintain the *status quo*. With hindsight, given what happened to Charles I, it can be seen to have been particularly perceptive. And for those who wish to argue that Cecil was more of a statesman than has often been thought, there is the fact that he almost always acted on his own advice over a period of 40 years - with the notable exception of his treatment of the Northern Earls during the

1560s. Camden, writing within a few decades of his death, summarised Cecil's approach well. He wrote that his aim had been 'to content the people with justice and favourable government which is not to exact frequent payments nor molest them with innovations'.

d) Dealings with the Queen

Cecil has often been portrayed as Elizabeth's faithful retainer - as a sort of male 'nanny' figure. He has been seen at the start of the reign as filling the role of the elder brother she never had (he was 13 years her senior), and to have progressively become her dog's-body, constantly at her beck and call and allowed little time to himself, even when he was painfully unwell or when a member of his immediate family had recently died. Two of the most often quoted pieces of contemporary evidence refer to their relationship. Part of the queen's speech on appointing him her Secretary in 1558 is reported as being:

'This judgment I have of you that you will not be corrupted with any manner of gift, and that you will be faithful to the state, and that without respect of my private will you will give me that counsel that you think best.

Cecil wrote, as he did on so many issues, about what he perceived his role as being.

1 As long as I may be allowed to give advice, I will not change my opinion by affirming the contrary, for that were to offend God, to whom I am sworn first, but as a servant I will obey her Majesty's commandment, and no wise contrary the same, presuming she
5 being God's chief minister here, it shall be God's will to have her commandments obeyed, after that I have performed my duty as a counsellor and shall in my heart wish her commandments to have such good success as I am sure she intendeth.

This picture of the honest servant fearlessly giving advice and humbly accepting his mistress's decision whatever it may be was for a long time accepted by historians as a fair approximation to the truth. The relationship was presented as a truly hierarchical one, with Elizabeth not only being 'top dog' but also having wisdom on her side. The point was perhaps made most starkly by Camden when he wrote of Elizabeth that, 'she had so rare gifts, as when her counsellors had said all they could say, she would frame out a wise counsel beyond all theirs'.

Then the historical pendulum swung. As it became clear that Cecil was not just the provider of advice and executor of the queen's wishes, the idea that he was possibly the power behind the throne gained ground. Plenty of evidence came to light which showed that the

Secretary regularly attempted to manipulate Elizabeth. Letters were found in which he told English ambassadors abroad what to include in their reports so that the queen would be fed a version of events that supported the policy which Cecil wished to see pursued. Reinterpretations of the parliamentary agitations of 1563 and 1566 over the succession (see page 106) made it clear that they were orchestrated by Cecil in an attempt to pressurise Elizabeth into accepting the way forward that he advocated. Most tellingly of all, it was shown that Cecil sometimes conspired with his fellow councillors in the hope of forcing his will on the queen by making her accept a course of action which she had explicitly expressed herself to be against. This definitely happened in 1559 when the aim was to bring about armed intervention in Scotland in favour of the Protestants and against Mary, Queen of Scots. It also occurred in the 1580s once Cecil had reached the conclusion that the execution of Mary, Queen of Scots was essential to the security of the realm. It was even suggested that Cecil's way of working was to decide on the policy he wished to pursue and then to think up ways of persuading Elizabeth to accept it.

As with most corrective interpretations, this revision of the relationship between Cecil and Elizabeth did two things. It highlighted the fact that the then current orthodoxy was seriously flawed, especially in that it was grossly oversimplified, and it indicated the direction in which the truth almost certainly lies. But, as so often happens, it is also clear that the 'correction' was overdone - that the pendulum swung too far in the opposite direction. Although there is no doubt that at times Cecil was the instigator of policy and Elizabeth was the victim of manipulation, the norm was definitely that the Secretary presented the queen with the advice he knew she wanted to hear. This was partly because their approaches to many issues - especially religion and warfare - were very similar, but it was also significantly because Cecil recognised that unwelcome advice would not only be ignored, but would also attract royal displeasure. It is also the case that Cecil was more often than not unsuccessful when he attempted to conduct an independent policy. Very often he was defeated by Elizabeth's standard ploy of refusing to make a decision - which was effective except on the small number of occasions when Cecil wished to stop her taking action - but he sometimes came painfully unstuck when the queen discovered what her faithful servant was doing. Cecil seems to have visibly wilted when faced by one of his mistress's temper tantrums. Thus it seems that the queen mainly led and that her minister mainly followed. It is true that Cecil took the initiative more often than was once thought, but it also appears that his success rate when he did so was not high. More often than not, all he could do was to argue his case with humility as frequently as he was allowed to, and to hope that eventually a decision might be made in his favour. As he was said to have advised the Earl of Essex on the subject of handling the queen, 'Good my Lord, overcome her with yielding, without disparagement of your honour, and plead your own cause with your presence'. He knew that little could be achieved without patience and persistence.

3 Lord Robert Dudley, Earl of Leicester

a) Background

Leicester, like Cecil, was a member of the third generation of a family of courtiers. But there the similarity ceased. The Dudleys did everything that the Cecils avoided doing. They played for high stakes, risking all in the process, and often lost. Leicester's grandfather, Sir Edmund Dudley, had allowed himself to become the public face of Henry VII's unpopular financial policy and had paid for his foolhardiness with his life once his protector was dead. His father had risen to a dukedom (Northumberland) and to becoming the effective ruler of the country, but had taken one risk too many when he attempted to place his daughter-in-law, Lady Jane Grey, on the throne. As was his father before him, he was executed for treason. When he died in 1553 he left five sons behind him. By 1558 this number had been reduced to two, the younger of whom, Lord Robert, had established himself as one of the Princess Elizabeth's closest friends. He was probably of the same age as her (there is an unsubstantiated tradition that they were born on the same day), and as the new queen's contemporary he was able to establish himself as one of her confidants rather than as one of her advisers.

Dudley's initial role was as a courtier, a member of Elizabeth's household, rather than as a politician or an administrator. From the beginning of the reign he served as the queen's Master of Horse. This was a prestigious position in that it kept him in daily contact with his mistress, as he made the arrangements both for her frequent hunting expeditions and for her routine transportation from place to place. It was obvious from the outset that the two of them revelled in each other's company. Although the queen seemed from time to time to lose her heart to other men, she regularly returned to her 'Robin' once each infatuation had run its course. There is no doubt that she loved him deeply and that during the winter of 1559-60 she came close to marrying him (see page 102). It is likely that she then resolved never to marry and that she henceforth (with one exception in 1579) contented herself with a long-running platonic affair with Dudley, interspersed with equally non-physical relationships with a sequence of favourites. Many writers have speculated about whether she was literally the 'Virgin Queen' of tradition. The evidence, unsurprisingly, is inconclusive, but it seems likely that any 'indiscretions' she committed would have been infrequent, spur-of-the-moment (and historically insignificant) lapses. Anything else would have been virtually impossible to conceal given the public nature of even the most personal aspects of her private life.

It rapidly became apparent to those at Court that Dudley was too ambitious to remain for long as merely the queen's 'good friend'. He wished for status, wealth and power. The way in which Elizabeth handled these yearnings has been the subject of universally complimentary comment. It is judged that she managed his translation from courtier to leading politician and minister with consummate skill. Not only did she effect the change by stages over several years (Dudley had to wait until 1562 to become a Privy Councillor and 1564 to become a peer, as Earl of Leicester), but she took positive steps to smooth the ruffled feathers that the promotion of her favourite was likely to cause. On the day that Dudley was made a Councillor, the same honour was extended to the Duke of Norfolk, as the premier peer of the realm. The clear message was being given that the promotion of 'new men' was not happening at the expense of the old aristocracy. At the same time Cecil was left in no doubt that he was in no way being superseded. Equally as important, the queen took great care to establish the fact that she was not unduly influenced by her favourite. She granted him sufficient land and other sources of income to allow him to maintain himself in the style of a leading nobleman - for he had little wealth of his own - but she made a public show of not conceding to his every wish. Most dramatically she even seized a knife and slashed to pieces the patent creating him an earl when it was first brought to her. In the end she made him wait several years for the title on which he had set his heart.

b) The Man

Leicester has received a very bad press from historians over the centuries. Many of the judgements of him have been unbalanced in their hostility. An honourable exception to the trend was the assessment made by William Camden, which was possibly written during Elizabeth's reign, although it was not published until after she had died. This verdict is a good example of Camden's remarkable skill (for his time) as a historian.

> 1 He was esteemed a most accomplished courtier, spruce and neat, free and bountiful to soldiers and students, a cunning time server and respecter of his own advantages, of a disposition ready and apt to please, crafty and subtle towards his adversaries, much given
> 5 formerly to women, and in his latter days doting extremely upon marriage. But whilst he preferred power and greatness ... before solid virtue, his detracting emulators found large matter to speak reproachfully of him, and even when he was in his most flourishing condition spared not disgracefully to defame him by libels, not
> 10 without mixture of some untruths. In a word, people talked openly in his commendation, but privately he was ill spoken of by the greater part.

But it is to be noticed that even though Camden was struggling to be fair, he could only find three complimentary things to say about Leicester. There is no doubt that he was an immensely accomplished courtier by any standard and that he put all his English contemporaries in the shade. He lavished flattery and attention on Elizabeth almost unceasingly (he rarely took time off from his 'work'), and he was expert in making the grand gesture. He displayed his expertise most strikingly in 1575 when he entertained the queen and the court at Kenilworth, his

Earl of Leicester c 1575-80, artist unknown

home in Warwickshire. No expense was spared in laying on a sequence of feasts and entertainments, including a subsequently famed water pageant in which huge representations of sea creatures accompanied the reciters of appropriately sycophantic poems. The event was still remembered decades later and may even have been the basis of part of Shakespeare's *A Midsummer Night's Dream.* Leicester was also 'spruce and neat' if by that is meant that he dressed extravagantly well. In an age when men's attire was if anything even more flamboyant than women's, Leicester outshone all his fellow courtiers with his costly outfits. His clothes generally incorporated more jewels, were made up of a greater range of fine materials, and were more exquisitely designed than those of any of his rivals. He was also renowned for the splendour of his gifts, although it would be a mistake to imagine that his liberality arose from any generosity of spirit. Leicester lived in an age when one measure of status was the size and spread of the gifts a person distributed and he well knew how to create the right impression. He was especially careful to scatter his largesse where it would be most noticed and talked about. Visitors from abroad, especially from France, frequently returned home with a flatteringly large present, and were subsequently likely to be found praising the greatness of the Queen of England's leading courtier.

However, it is not surprising that none of Leicester's supposedly positive qualities smacked of virtue as it would be difficult to argue by any ethical standard that he was a good man. It appears that he was completely self-centred, placing nobody and no cause above what he perceived to be his own interest. His friendships lasted only as long as he found them advantageous and he was not committed from principle to any of the policies he espoused. He rightly earned and retained a reputation for being undependable. The fact that he was relatively so powerful and influential makes it very appropriate for him to be described metaphorically as a loose cannon - it was possible that he would 'go off' in any direction and that he would damage his friends as much as his foes. He was arrogant and took offence where none was intended. Because he was also spiteful and small-minded he was a very dangerous man to cross. He would go out of his way to damage the interests of even the lowly if they earned his displeasure. On one occasion the civic dignitaries of Warwick failed, through a misunder-standing over arrangements, to provide him with the welcome that he considered to be his due, and his reaction was not only petulant at the time. Subsequently he sought opportunities to blacken the name of the town wherever he could.

In many ways Leicester was a typical bully, throwing his weight about when he thought he could get away with it but acting like a coward when he suspected that he was in a losing position. In many ways he showed his true colours when he escaped from Elizabeth's apron strings for a prolonged period during 1585, 1586 and 1587 while leading the English army in the Netherlands (see John Warren's volume in the series for the background to this situation). Not only did he act like a spoiled *prima donna* but he also blatantly ignored the queen's explicit instructions whenever he thought he could do so with impunity. He accepted personal rewards and dignities, although he must have understood that in doing so he was undermining the policy he had been sent to implement. He was reckless in giving out the message that he knew better than a 'mere woman'. It is little wonder that Elizabeth was furious with frustration over her temporary powerlessness to control her favourite, who of course was predictably meek and apologetic when he was once more within her grasp. Leicester had displayed a similar tendency to take up an untenable position and then to back down unreservedly in 1569 during the complex series of interrelated plottings aimed at discrediting Cecil and bringing about the marriage of the Duke of Norfolk with Mary, Queen of Scots. He joined with the conspirators when it seemed that their endeavours might be successful but as soon as it became apparent that the queen knew what was happening and was determined to oppose it, he abandoned his colleagues, told all that he knew, and successfully begged for forgiveness. Norfolk was equally cowardly but was slower to disassociate himself from the plot. He eventually paid for his stupidity with his life. The Earls of Northumberland and Westmorland were panicked into hopeless rebellion and thereby utterly ruined themselves and their families.

Elements of the same behaviour were apparent in Leicester's actions over his own marital prospects. After 1561 he probably knew in his heart of hearts that Elizabeth would never marry him, although he continued to harbour the hope that he might be wrong. His dilemma was that on the one hand the queen was most jealous of his affections, throwing violent temper tantrums if he paid attention to anybody else, while on the other hand he needed to contract a legal marriage if he was to fulfil his strongly held ambition to father children who would continue the Dudley line. On several occasions he came close to risking his monarch's disfavour by forming a permanent liaison but thought better of it at the last moment. He even turned his back on the virtual certainty of successful parenthood when he disowned the noble widow who was carrying his child - some have claimed that he had in fact been through a secret marriage ceremony with the lady, who illegitimately bore him the healthy son whom he so deeply desired. In 1578 he at last plucked up sufficient courage to risk Elizabeth's ultimate disfavour by marrying, although he hoped to have his cake and eat it by swearing to secrecy all those who knew that Lettice Knollys, dowager Countess of Essex, was now his wife. But he had given up a hostage to fortune. His political opponents got wind of what had happened and in 1579 alerted the queen to the situation at just the moment the news was likely to stampede her into the French match they wished her to accept (see page 114). In the event the strategy misfired. The French marriage did not take place and a suitably contrite Leicester was eventually restored to royal favour, although at the cost of being almost permanently separated from his wife who was decidedly *persona non grata* at court. In 1588 on Leicester's death, Elizabeth allowed herself one of her occasional bouts of spitefulness when she encouraged others to attempt to reduce the now dowager Countess of Leicester to penury.

c) The Politician

Leicester had two great strengths as a politician: his closeness to Queen Elizabeth, and his ability to make good use of royal favour. To employ a shooting metaphor, the latter was his gun and the former was his ammunition. He was a highly ambitious political leader and both of his strengths were essential if he was to achieve the success he desired - he wanted both to be the most powerful person in England after the queen and to be thought of as such.

During the 1560s Leicester struggled hard to achieve both of his ambitions, once it became clear at the start of the decade that success was not to come in one simple move by him marrying Elizabeth and becoming King-Consort. In order for him to become the most powerful political figure it would be necessary for him to eliminate, or at least to eclipse, Sir William Cecil. He attempted to do this by destroying the Secretary's credibility in the eyes of the queen. But because Cecil was so skilful in avoiding leaving himself open to criticism, Leicester was forced over and over again to resort to falsehood or gross misrepresentation in order to make it appear to Elizabeth that her Secretary had acted in such a manner that he should be replaced. In 1569 he went as far as telling the queen in front of witnesses that Cecil was so unpopular that civil war was likely to break out if he was not disgraced. But Elizabeth was resolute in her determination to stand by her leading servant and, much as Cecil was convinced from time to time that all was lost, she refused to dispense with his services. At the same time she was careful to assure her favourite that his position was also secure. Leicester was granted a steady stream of honours, of positions of local influence, and of income-bearing leases and licences. He was also allowed to give his advice, although it was not always followed, on all major issues of policy. He was therefore firmly established as one of the queen's leading ministers, although he was denied his desire of becoming more important than anyone else.

By the mid-1560s Leicester was clearly seen to be one of the most powerful men in the land. This was evidenced by his ability to secure for his followers a whole range of positions and privileges by the exercise of patronage. At the lower levels of the system he was able to make grants to people because of the positions, such as Chancellor of Oxford University, he held himself and because he was able to request his senior supporters to dispose of posts in their gift in the way he desired. But the most important element of his power as a patron and leader of a major faction was the influence he exercised with the queen. He was widely and accurately perceived as the person, along with Cecil, most likely to be able to persuade her to appoint his favoured candidate to any vacant position of significance. The fact that even he generally found it very difficult to prevail on Elizabeth to make an appointment he desired without persistent cajoling over a long period did not lessen his standing as a provider of patronage because it was recognised that others fared even less well than he did.

However, it was in his attempt to be accepted by the leaders of other factions as the preeminent political figure that caused Leicester the greatest difficulty. His rapid rise and his overbearing manner led to his being detested by many members of the 'old' aristocracy. But only one member of this group, the Earl of Sussex, had both the personality and the standing to challenge the political domination of the queen's favourite. He, very often followed by the Duke of Norfolk, resisted Leicester's pretensions at every turn. He regarded Cecil as the person most likely to steer the ship of state safely through the troubled waters of international friction and internal divisions. He looked upon Leicester as a pretentious upstart who spelled nothing but trouble and he sought out every opportunity to challenge the new man and, if possible, to put him down. In a society in which ancestry meant so much his most telling jibe at Leicester's expense was that only two of his forefathers were known and that both of them had been executed for treason. The fact that neither Sussex nor Leicester would give way to the other gave rise to a sequence of very petty but very public squabbles between 1564 and 1569. Such was the ferocity of many of these confrontations, with each leader calling upon their followers to identify themselves and to snub the supporters of the other, that the orthodox view among historians in the first half of the twentieth century was that Elizabethan politics was characterised by faction fighting. Some even maintained that the rivalry between the two main factions was so intense that the country came close to dissolving into civil war. Although it is now generally agreed that the first view was misleading and that the second was a considerable exaggeration, there is no doubt that the Leicester-Sussex rivalry was a potentially destabilising feature of the politics of the 1560s, and was a contest in which there were no winners.

There is only circumstantial evidence to support the view that Leicester learnt from his unsuccessful attempt both to be and to be seen to be England's leading political figure, but it is persuasive. The last time he attempted to oust his rivals by indulging in metaphorical political assassination was in 1569. Thereafter he co-operated more often than he challenged and he employed less extreme measures in his attempts to win the queen's support for the policies he championed. It was this change of attitude that has been largely responsible for historians coming to think of the 1570s as the period of mid-reign political stability. This view does not maintain that there was a consensus on all issues, but that there was agreement among all the leading politicians (mainly between Leicester and Cecil) that the top priority was to maintain the security of the régime. Thus the major divisive issue of the period - whether or not England should become the leader of international Protestantism, in particular by providing armed assistance to the Dutch rebels in their fight against Philip II - was never allowed to become a life and death struggle between the advocates of each side. Thus the 'forward' party, led by Leicester and Sir Francis Walsingham (Secretary from 1573 to 1590) and the 'cautious' party, led by Cecil,

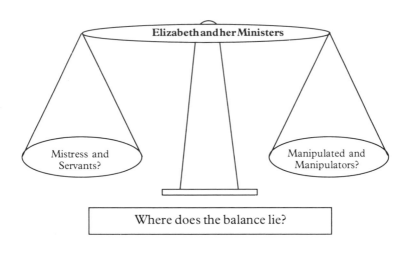

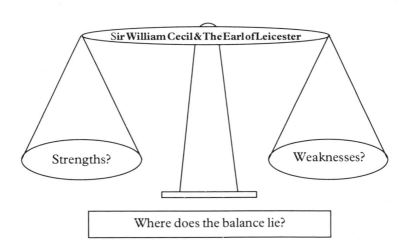

Summary - Elizabeth and her Servants

employed a wide range of dirty tricks - mainly involving the spreading of misinformation - in an effort to gain success for their cause, but there was no attempted coup as there had been in 1569. When Leicester died in 1588 Elizabeth lost her long-time best friend and the major adornment of her court. England lost a leading (but not its leading) politician who had changed from being the wild man of the 1560s into being a supporter of the status quo in his later years. He left a gap that, in the event, could not be filled, with consequences which will be explored in chapter 7.

Making notes on 'Elizabeth and her Servants'

This is an important chapter from a note making point of view because it contains a large amount of information which you are likely to need when answering examination questions. The notes you make are therefore likely to be extensive.

Part of the task should be relatively straightforward. You need to be prepared to answer questions on Cecil and Leicester, either singly or in combination. For this you require basic factual information about the life and career of each man, and ideas to use when assessing both men in a variety of ways (importance, as statesmen, etc). The simplest way of assembling such material is to make notes on the relevant sections of the chapter, using the headings that appear in the text.

The second part of the task is much more complicated. The aim here is to assemble notes from which you will be able to prepare yourself to answer questions about the relationship between Elizabeth and her ministers. Before doing this you need to decide which historical issue or issues will provide the framework of your notes. Your best bet will probably be to concentrate on the issue of the nature of the relationship (mistress and servants? manipulated and manipulators? equal partners? etc). The most effective way to do this is to make notes in three sections, under headings such as 'Elizabeth dominant', 'Ministers dominant' and 'Conclusion'. Have separate sheets of paper for each section and gather together your notes under the first two headings as you re-read the chapter. Once you have done this you will be ready to think out what judgement to make in the third section.

Answering essay questions on 'Elizabeth and her Servants'

It is possible that you will be asked a question about Burghley, or about Burghley and Leicester, or (more rarely) about Leicester on his own. It will be worthwhile preparing to answer all three types of question. Look at the following examples.

1   How far was Elizabeth I's great confidence in Lord Burghley

justified?

2   Assess the part played by the Earl of Leicester in Elizabethan politics.

3   Compare and contrast Lord Burghley and the Earl of Leicester as 'servants of the crown'.

4   Evaluate the work of Sir William Cecil (Lord Burghley) as Queen Elizabeth's leading minister between 1558 and 1598.

5   Has the Earl of Leicester been unfairly treated by historians?

6   'Lord Burghley was all substance while the Earl of Leicester was all show.' Discuss.

Although the wording of the four questions that concentrate on Burghley or Leicester individually differs greatly, the task the candidate is being asked to undertake in each case is very similar. What is this common element shared by the questions? Equally, questions 3 and 6 are setting the same type of task. What is this?

The key to tackling questions such as 1, 2, 4, and 5 successfully is the selection of the criteria according to which the assessment is to be made. Sometimes the criteria are suggested by the wording of the question (as they are in question 1) but more often than not the candidate is left to choose them for him or herself. Because this is such a common situation it is sensible to enter the examination room with clearly thought out ideas about the criteria to be used in making different types of assessment. There is no 'right' answer in the choice of criteria - there are as many acceptable 'sets' as there are reasonable views about the nature of history itself. From an examiner's point of view what is important is that a candidate has reached clear decisions about the issue and that this clarity is apparent in what is written. If you have not yet made decisions about the criteria you will use to assess historical figures now is perhaps the time to do so. Most people find that this is best done in discussion with others.

Of course, the subject matter of this chapter also lends itself to questions about the relationship between Elizabeth and her ministers. However these are worded, most of them are likely to be of the 'how far/to what extent?' type, as are the following.

7   Did Elizabeth I control her ministers or did they control her?

8   Was Elizabeth I the effective head of her own government?

9   Who decided government policy in Elizabethan England?

Make brief plans for answers to questions 7-9 so as to show that they are of the 'how far/to what extent?' type.

Source-based questions on 'Elizabeth and her Servants'

1 Elizabeth and Cecil

Carefully read the two extracts on the relationship between Elizabeth and Sir William Cecil, given on page 63. Answer the following questions.

a) In your own words describe the three judgements that, in the first extract, Elizabeth said she had made of Cecil. (6 marks)
b) In the second extract what is meant by 'I will not change my opinion by affirming the contrary'? (2 marks)
c) What can be learned about Elizabeth from the first extract? (6 marks)
d) Suggest three ways in which Cecil did not live up to the standards described in the second extract. Illustrate each of the 'ways' with an example. (6 marks)

2 Camden on Leicester

Carefully read Camden's assessment of Leicester given on page 66. Answer the following questions.

a) What is meant by 'crafty and subtle towards his adversaries'? (2 marks)
b) What evidence does the extract contain to support the view that Camden was attempting to be objective in his assessment? (3 marks)
c) What is Camden's opinion of Leicester? Explain your answer. (5 marks)

3 Portraits of Cecil and Leicester

Study the portraits of Cecil and Leicester on pages 54 and 67. Answer the following questions.

a) Compare and contrast the portraits. (10 marks)
b) In what ways do the portraits substantiate what is known about the personalities and values of the two men? (10 marks)
    Do not include any of the same points in the answers to both question a) and question b).

CHAPTER 5

Elizabeth and Parliament

1 Introduction

We have already seen that the words 'government' and 'servant' had very different meanings in the second half of the sixteenth century to those of today. The same is true of the word 'parliament'. It is important to keep this fact continuously in mind while studying this chapter. Otherwise there will be the danger of slipping into the trap of imagining that the Elizabethan parliamentary system closely resembled the modern one. This is especially easily done because there are many superficial similarities between the two. In both the organisation is into two houses - the Lords made up of peers (barons, viscounts, earls, marquesses, and dukes) and Church of England archbishops and bishops who are members as of right; and the Commons made up of members (MPs) who represent geographically defined constituencies. In both, new laws are made in essentially the same way - they are introduced as 'bills', are agreed on three occasions by each House, and are accepted by the monarch, whereupon they change from being 'bills' to being 'acts of parliament'. In both, the monarch is a part of parliament, although separate from the two houses, only appearing there (invariably in the Lords) on formal occasions such as the opening or the dissolution of a parliament.

However, it must be remembered that these similarities merely mask the fact that in almost all essentials the late-sixteenth century parliamentary system was fundamentally different from the modern one. We are used to a situation in which parliament, as represented by the House of Commons, lies at the heart of the nation's political life. Votes taken there decide the fate of governments and their policies and there is an official opposition party which plays the part of a government-in-waiting. Parliament is continually (allowing for holidays) in session, and each parliament is almost immediately followed by another one, divided only by a hotly contested general election in which MPs are chosen and the complexion of the next government is normally decided. The House of Lords rarely plays a significant part in events, and the monarch is merely a non-political figurehead.

The situation faced by Elizabeth I could hardly have been more different. She (and not parliament) was firmly at the heart of the nation's political life. The government (if by this we mean the Privy Council - see page 33) was responsible to her alone, and parliament played no part in either its selection or its policy making. The House of Lords was at least as important as the House of Commons, which is not surprising as, for example, over a third of MPs were effectively nominated by powerful lords. To speak of 'elections' is probably misleading. The vast majority of MPs were 'returned' rather than 'elected', in that their nomination was uncontested, meaning that there was no need for a vote to be taken. In fact, parliament was an occasional and peripheral part of the political system. It met only when and for as long as the queen wished it to. As a result there were only 13 sessions of parliament (1559, 1563, 1566, 1571, 1572, 1576, 1581, 1584, 1586, 1589, 1593, 1597 and 1601) during the more than 44 years of Elizabeth's reign, and no session lasted for more than a few months. And even while it was in session its activities were severely circumscribed by generally accepted custom and practice. Its primary function was undoubtedly to consider whatever issues (normally in the form of bills) the queen's representatives asked it to, and, as loyal subjects, to give assent to whatever was proposed. It was expected that, in the Commons in particular, any querying of the queen's intentions would be moderate, cautious and highly respectful. Although it was universally agreed that members of either House were free to initiate draft legislation - in fact, the majority of bills considered by parliament were introduced by MPs who were pursuing private or local interests - it was widely understood that some issues were 'taboo'.

Unfortunately for the smooth running of parliament, there were differences of opinion about what was 'off limits' and what was not. Elizabeth was one of the few people who had no doubts on the matter. She drew a clear distinction between those subjects which touched on her prerogative (and were therefore not to be discussed in parliament except by invitation) and those that had to do with the commonweal (which fell within parliament's competence). In practice she viewed almost all issues of national importance as falling within her prerogative - religion (because this was her responsibility as God's representative on earth), foreign policy (because this had to do with dealings between princes, in which subjects should not interfere), how she spent her money, whether she married, who should succeed her, and whom she should favour (because these were personal matters which were nobody's business but hers). Although many of her leading subjects thought that Elizabeth was reserving too much to herself, they were almost all reluctantly prepared to respect her wishes for almost all of the time. When they did not, sparks were likely to fly.

There were no parties and therefore no party politics in parliament. The nearest approach to organised groupings (excepting Neale's 'Puritan Choir' - see page 80) that existed were the temporary 'connexions' of MPs who owed their election to a particular parliament to the influence of the same leading politician. The best known example of this phenomenon was the collection of over 30 MPs who can be shown to have been the clients of the Earl of Essex in the 1590s. However, such groupings had virtually nothing in common with modern-day political parties. There is no evidence that their members felt any sense of group identity or that any attempt was made to arrange for them to work or to vote in unison. It seems that the major effort that some court politicians made from time to time to ensure the election of as many of their followers as possible was no more than one part of an attempt to demonstrate that they wielded more influence than was possessed by their rivals. Thus the acquiring of control of parliamentary seats was an end in itself and not the prelude to subsequent collective action once parliament met. This was hardly surprising given that the way in which parliament worked gave little scope for any form of party politics. It is true that Burghley ensured that a handful of his servants sat in each parliament in order to see to the business of nursing government bills through the necessary procedures, but these men did not constitute a party in any meaningful sense of the word.

2 How Historians have Approached the Topic

Serious academic research on the history of the reign of Elizabeth I began in the middle of the nineteenth century. At the time Britain was in the process of developing from a parliamentary monarchy into a fully-fledged parliamentary democracy, and it is therefore hardly surprising that considerable interest was shown in identifying the part that the years 1558-1603 played in shifting the balance of power from the monarch to the two houses of parliament, and especially the House of Commons. This was particularly so because one of the main benefits of studying history was thought to be the acquisition of an understanding of how the present came to be as it was. This went hand in hand with a belief in 'progress' - an assumption that history told the story of a step-by-step improvement in all aspects of life, leading to the pinnacle of the present and destined to continue in the same direction into the indefinite future. These attitudes lay at the heart of what is normally referred to as 'the Whig view of history'. They were accepted by the vast majority of British academic historians until some years after the Second World War.

The consensus among Whig historians was that, although Elizabeth's reign witnessed the first tentative steps by MPs to break free from the stifling control of the monarch, the struggle between Crown and Commons only began in earnest after 1603. It was maintained that the Elizabethan parliaments were typified by their members' ready acceptance of the queen's dominance and superiority. Given this situation, it was only to be expected that the spotlight of researchers' attention would be turned onto the dealings between Elizabeth and her parliaments in an attempt to discover evidence that the origins of the breakdown in relations that was to lead to the outbreak of the Civil War could be clearly identified in the Tudor period. It was therefore no great surprise - although it was a dramatic departure from the prevailing orthodoxy - when one of the major themes in the account of the history of parliament in Elizabeth's reign published by J.E. (later Sir John) Neale in the 1950s turned out to be the attempt made by an organised group within the House of Commons to increase parliamentary powers and privileges in the face of stout resistance from the Crown.

The Neale interpretation almost immediately established itself as the new orthodoxy. It was almost inevitable that this would happen. Not only was Neale a high quality and much respected historian - one of the foremost figures in the British historical 'establishment' of his time - who had presented a well-substantiated case based on large-scale research, but his findings also fitted in well with most people's expectations of what would be discovered. For just about a generation (until the early-1980s) it was generally accepted that what was effectively the last word on the issue had been written. However, during the period of the Neale orthodoxy two unconnected trends developed which taken together raised doubts about the wisdom of regarding the topic as having been settled once and for all. Little by little the Whig view of history was challenged and discredited, until by about 1970 it was widely regarded as being old fashioned. Although no alternative 'view' took over as a new orthodox approach to studying the past, it became commonplace to stress the dangers of historical hindsight, especially when deciding the 'angle' from which to study a topic. One result of this was that many historians became convinced that topics and issues should be explored within the context of their own times, rather than being used primarily to provide explanations for subsequent events. The second trend was much more specific. Historians interested in the causes of the Civil War of the 1640s started to question whether long-term causes were as important as had traditionally been thought. By the mid-1980s it was generally agreed that there was no need to look back beyond 1637 to discover the most significant causes of the war. The cumulative effect of these two trends was to make it look as if Neale had been asking the wrong questions when he carried out his research on the Elizabethan parliaments, resulting in an unbalanced account of events being given.

The realisation that Neale had presented a lop-sided picture of Elizabethan parliamentary history was sufficient to ensure that the topic would be re-examined. However, the need to do so was put beyond question in the early 1980s when a number of historians (notably Norman Jones, M.A.R. Graves, and Sir Geoffrey Elton) almost simultaneously published well supported claims that Neale had misunderstood the key pieces of evidence upon which his main case was founded. It was then shown that nearly all his supporting evidence was unreliable, as the conclusions that he had drawn from it were often dubious and were sometimes clearly untenable. Rarely has such a well established historical interpretation collapsed so rapidly and so completely. Almost overnight what had seemed certain was generally agreed to be mistaken, and the way was thrown open for fresh interpretations to establish themselves. Recent research, especially by Elton, has largely filled the void, although there is still a need for more work to be done.

3 The Neale Interpretation

The phrase that is most closely associated with Neale's work on the Elizabethan Parliament is 'the Puritan Choir'. This was used to describe the group of Puritan MPs which Neale identified as working together in an attempt to force Elizabeth to adopt policies that were to its members' liking and to raise the status of the House of Commons by formalising its procedures and strengthening its privileges. Neale had been made aware of the group when he came across a contemporary pamphlet which named 43 of the MPs of 1566 and described them individually in satirical terms as forming the members of a Puritan choir. Armed with this list of names, he was able to identify numerous occasions on which one or more members of the group opposed the queen's wishes, championed the rights of the Commons, or made an effort to change the laws regulating religion so as to make the Church of England more Puritan. The Choir was credited with forcing Elizabeth in 1559 to adopt a more Protestant religious settlement than she really wanted, with stirring up trouble in 1563 and 1566 over the queen's failure to marry or to name a successor (see page 106), with scheming between 1563 and 1571 to bring about further reforms in the Church of England, and with agitating vigorously in 1572 for the execution of Mary, Queen of Scots, and the Duke of Norfolk, both of whom had been found guilty of plotting to force Elizabeth from the throne and, once having married, to rule the country in her place and presumably in the Catholic interest.

Not surprisingly, Neale made much of the times when MPs acted in a manner that foreshadowed events during the lead-up to the Civil War. He found it particularly significant that in 1566 the Commons attempted, for the first time on record, to postpone agreeing to the queen's request for money until she had satisfied their grievances. This strategy was not successful on this occasion but it was subsequently to be employed in 1640 with dramatic effect. Here seemed to be a clear-cut example of MPs starting to flex their collective muscles. Equally, the actions of the Wentworth brothers, Peter and Paul, in the parliaments between 1576 and 1593 were strongly highlighted. Peter was the real firebrand. He made speeches attacking Elizabeth for what he described as her mistaken policies, he championed changing the Church of England into a Puritan organisation, and he argued for the right of the House of Commons to be allowed to discuss whatever it wished and in whatever terms seemed appropriate to it. He was the stuff of which martyrs are made. He ignored warnings that he should moderate his conduct, including a month spent in the Tower on the orders of his fellow MPs, and eventually he tried Elizabeth's patience too far. In 1593 he was once more sent to the Tower. This time was no warning, and he remained there until he died four years later. As far as Neale was concerned there could hardly be clearer evidence of the struggle for power between the monarch and parliament's lower house.

4 The Corrective to Neale

Once, in the early 1980s, it became firmly established that Neale's 'Puritan Choir' was a figment of the imagination, based on a misunderstanding of the central piece of evidence, the entire edifice of the Neale interpretation came crashing down. More and more of the separate strands of the story, which Neale had woven together to form a coherent account of conflict between a conservative monarch and a radical-dominated House of Commons, were shown not to support the conclusions that had been drawn from them. Perhaps the most telling of these correctives was the revelation that some members of Neale's Puritan Choir (notably Thomas Norton and William Fleetwood) were in fact the followers and 'men of business' of members of the Privy Council (especially Burghley). It is true that they were sometimes found encouraging their fellow MPs to put pressure on Elizabeth to amend her policies and, in particular, to take action where she seemed reluctant to do so. But it has been convincingly argued that in doing so these 'choristers' were not acting as part of an organised and on-going grouping of radicals who wished to alter the balance of power between the Crown and Parliament in the House of Commons' favour, and fundamentally to reform the Church of England in order to move its beliefs and practices further from those of the Church of Rome. What is almost certainly the case - the evidence is largely circumstantial but is nevertheless highly convincing - is that these men were instructed to take the action they did by their political masters who were members of the queen's inner circle of advisers.

So what was going on? It appears that the happenings in the Commons were no more than an extension of what was taking place in the discussions between Elizabeth and her leading privy councillors. In fact, parliament was being used by the queen's increasingly frustrated ministers as an additional lever in their attempts to persuade their mistress to take action where she was proving extremely reluctant to do so. The major issues over which the Commons were used as an additional pressure-point were, in the 1560s, the queen's failure to marry or to nominate a successor, and, in the 1570s and early 1580s, her failure to take resolute action over the treasonable activities of Mary, Queen of Scots, or to lend effective support to the Dutch rebels. Burghley, in particular, hoped that if parliament joined in the chorus of pleadings for something to be done, Elizabeth would feel herself sufficiently cornered to decide that compliance with her ministers' advice was the lesser of all the evils. Such an explanation of the 'opposition' of, for example, Thomas Norton, who was presented by Neale as one of the leading lights of the Puritan Choir, is completely convincing as it appears to fit in with all the available evidence.

It is Elton who has gone furthest towards explaining the true significance of the 'Puritan Chorus' pamphlet of 1566 which Neale misinterpreted so badly. He has proved beyond doubt that it was not a celebration of 43 MPs who shared Puritan sympathies and most of whom had co-operated together since 1559, as they were in the years to come, in order to pressurise Elizabeth to adopt more radical policies. Not only was there the telling fact that about a dozen of the 43 were Privy Councillors, 'men of business' in the Commons, but it is also the case that few of the 'choir' deserved the epithet of 'Puritan'. Some even had clearly Catholic leanings, while Thomas Norton (singled out by Neale as the archetypal Puritan) was no more than a Protestant of moderate beliefs, although with a virulent hatred of Rome. But the mystery has not been completely solved. Whereas it has been possible to show what the pamphlet was not, it has not been possible to establish for certain what it was. It is very likely that the 43 MPs listed in the pamphlet were the members of a committee appointed to consult with representatives of the House of Lords on matters of common interest - a claim largely based on the fact that the same number of MPs, in addition to Privy Councillors, served on the committee as were named as members of the Puritan Choir - but no convincing explanation has been found for either the writing of a satire about the committee or the publication of it in an age when printing was a costly and time-consuming business. While this degree of uncertainty remains, there is always the theoretical possibility (unlikely as it may seem) that the 'Puritan Choir' will re-emerge as the cornerstone of another interpretation of the politics of the early-Elizabethan parliaments.

Although his interpretation has been so discredited that there is no possibility of it being reinstated, it should not be imagined that Neale's work is now considered to be worthless. It is true that his overview representation of the relations between Elizabeth and her parliaments as being characterised by conflict and tension is no longer held to be accurate, but some of the specific insights he provided into the parliamentary politics of the reign are still considered to be of value. There is no doubt that there was, from time to time, considerable discontent among MPs over the queen's actions (or lack of them). It has to be admitted that in the 1560s and 1570s, when the main 'opposition' was over Elizabeth's failure to marry, the succession, the Duke of Norfolk, and Mary, Queen of Scots, the agitation was orchestrated by members of the Privy Council. Nevertheless there must have been a large amount of latent discontent over the queen's reluctance to act, otherwise it would not have been possible for such large-scale storms of verbal protest to be whipped up. In addition, Neale was undoubtedly correct in claiming that, in the 1570s and 1580s at least, a number of MPs worked very hard in an attempt to persuade their colleagues that the Church of England should be made more Protestant, and that the 'liberties' of parliament should include the right to discuss whatever MPs wanted whenever they liked and in whatever terms they thought appropriate. It is also clear that this self-generated challenging of government policy reached its height in the vociferous anti-monopolies agitation of 1601 (see page 92). Where Neale got it wrong was in according the agitators greater numerical strength, organisation and significance that they actually possessed. There seems to be little possibility that there will be any substantial modification of the currently accepted view of the 'opposition' as being very small (no more than a handful of MPs at any one time), unorganised (with no evidence of concerted action planned on anything but a day-to-day basis), and of no long-term significance (in that it was not part of a process of deteriorating relations between monarch and parliament which culminated in the outbreak of civil war in 1642).

There is a danger of assuming that because Neale was so mistaken on major issues he was a poor historian. This would be an absurd and very unfair assumption to make. Neale spent nearly all of a long and distinguished working life researching and writing about the reign of Elizabeth. One sign of the lasting quality of what he wrote is that his biography of Elizabeth, although it was published more than 60 years ago, is still widely regarded as the most appropriate of the many books on the last of the Tudors for the serious student to consult when commencing an in-depth study of the period. Most of his work (other than his conclusions about the relationship between Elizabeth and the House of Commons) has stood the test of time well. However, it is necessary for the modern reader to be aware of the assumption of English superiority that lies behind many of the judgements he makes. It is therefore particularly important when enjoying reading Neale to have one's critical faculties 'engaged'.

How was it then that such an eminent historian was so wide of the mark when fashioning an explanation of the relations between Elizabeth and her parliaments? As far as is known, nobody has attempted to identify the stages by which this happened, but it seems likely that Neale fell into the trap which is probably the most difficult one for research historians to avoid. Having thought out a plausible hypothesis (that the origins of the conflict between parliament and the crown were to be found in the later-sixteenth century), he discovered plenty of evidence that appeared to support his emerging interpretation. Instead of rigorously examining this evidence to see whether interpretations other than his initial one were the most convincing, he allowed himself to believe that his findings pointed in the direction he had come to expect. All historians select and interpret evidence (it is only antiquarians who attempt to record all that they find), and the greatest difficulty facing them is to avoid pouncing on every fact that seems to support an explanation that they favour, while overlooking those that do not. Of course, the danger becomes even greater once the interpretation seems to have substance. Then new evidence that appears to give additional support to the preferred general explanation tends to be accepted with less-than-detailed scrutiny. It is perhaps a counsel of perfection to suggest that researchers should positively seek other explanations of their evidence even when several years of work have strongly indicated that a particular interpretation 'holds water', but it is the only way of avoiding the enormity of mistake such as the one that Neale made. Hundreds of other professional historians have acted as Neale did, and this helps to place the 'mistake' in context, even if it cannot justify it.

Many present-day historians would claim that earlier generations of, especially Whig, historians increased their vulnerability to the 'blinkered research' trap by attempting to read history backwards, in that they studied a period in the light of what was to follow and unthinkingly assumed that the only possible outcome of events was that which actually occurred. Of course, it could be argued that this is a large part of the reason why Neale came unstuck. It is therefore not surprising that those who have produced the major correctives to the Neale interpretation have been careful to argue that parliament should be studied as an institution in the round, rather than as one aspect of Elizabethan politics. Elton, in particular, has done this. His claim has been that by studying all aspects of parliamentary life he has been able to place the politics in their proper context. In the process he has been able to establish that the norm was co-operation between crown and Commons (with the hiccups in the relationship being real but untypical and only to be expected), that the House of Lords was of much greater importance than Neale thought (being the scene of many parliamentary initiatives, especially after 1571 when Sir William Cecil 'moved upstairs' as Lord Burghley), and that the attempts made by the Commons to defend, and even to extend, its privileges were knee-jerk responses by MPs who were temporarily stung into action by being brought face to face with the inferiority of their position (rather than being caused by a lower house that was in some way 'coming of age').

5 Elizabeth's Attitude towards Parliament

The old orthodox view was that Elizabeth looked upon parliament favourably as one forum in which she could maintain contact with her loyal subjects, listening to their concerns and explaining (or having explained) her policies to them. This interpretation arose from the evidence that was most readily available to the early generations of historians who studied the late-Tudor period. Prominent among this was material from two types of printed source: so-say verbatim accounts of the speeches delivered by Elizabeth to parliament and to delegations from both Houses that attended on her at her request, and the memoirs of MPs who had been present on such occasions. Both sources portrayed the queen as a gracious sovereign who was pleased to have the opportunity to share her thoughts with the representatives of her people. There was no reason to doubt that the sentiments expressed reflected Elizabeth's real sentiments.

The writings of Neale and others during the 1930s, 1940s and 1950s established a new orthodoxy in which Elizabeth was characterised as disliking parliament very much. Of course, this interpretation naturally arose from the portrayal of relations between queen and Commons as being strained for much of the time. It was a well-rounded view that was supported by plentiful evidence, both direct and circumstantial. There are many reports of Elizabeth's unwillingness to summon a new parliament or to arrange for a new session of an existing one. It appears that without exception she had to be persuaded to agree to the calling of a parliamentary session. In almost every case (12 out of 13) the argument used by her advisers was the need to arrange for the raising of additional taxation to pay off either an existing or a predicted deficit. The only exception was in 1572, when half of the taxes voted in the previous year remained to be collected, and the argument used was the need to ensure the widest possible support for the government following the proven treachery of Mary, Queen of Scots, and the Duke of Norfolk. The claim that Elizabeth only consented to the summoning of parliament when the financial situation left her no alternative was strengthened by the fact that she quickly expressed regret that she had been persuaded against her better judgement to agree to the session of 1572. Not only was Elizabeth reluctant to consent to the calling of parliament but she was also eager to make the sessions short. She said as much on several occasions when opening a parliament. Although she gave her reasoning as concern for the welfare of members, who, she knew, would not wish to be taken from their normal activities for longer than was absolutely necessary, it was assumed that this was merely public-relations hypocrisy and that her real motives were selfish. The circumstantial evidence used to support this interpretation was largely a matter of common sense. It was asserted that the situation made it almost certain that Elizabeth's attitude to parliament would be negative. After all, apart from voting her the extraordinary revenue that she required, parliament was merely a cause of aggravation to the queen. A close watch had to be kept on the Commons either to head off or, failing that, to nip in the bud the activities of 'opposition' members who attempted to stir up trouble in almost every session. This was at best an unnecessary distraction and at worst a cause of considerable annoyance, and it could well have been done without. Clearly Elizabeth would have been happier had it never been necessary for parliament to meet.

The revisionist historians who have discredited the central tenets of Neale's interpretation of parliamentary history between 1558 and 1603 have also drawn attention to the need to submit his views on Elizabeth's attitude towards parliament to careful scrutiny. However, their plea has been for a measured modification rather than an outright rejection of the orthodox interpretation. At the heart of their case has been the warning that the general tenor of the Neale-line encourages people to exaggerate the extent of Elizabeth's negative feelings towards parliament. It is therefore thought to be important that some boundaries to the dislike are established. For example, there is no question that Elizabeth ever contemplated doing without parliament on a permanent basis, as Charles I was to do in the 1620s. Nor did the queen's desire for short sessions ever lead her to view parliament merely as the means of acquiring additional funds. She was never in a tearing hurry either to ensure the introduction and passage of the subsidy bill (the legislation agreeing to the taxation) at the beginning of a session or to dissolve parliament once the financial business had been done. An examination of the dates of the beginning and end of sessions and of the introduction and final acceptance of subsidy bills shows that Elizabeth was prepared to allow ample opportunities for other parliamentary business to be done. It is reasonable to conclude that, had the queen been as hostile to parliament as the Neale interpretation invites us to think she was, subsidy bills would always have been introduced within a few days of the start of a session and the session would have been brought to a close within a few days of the procedures granting the taxation having been completed. But this was not the case.

Of course, this is not to argue that Elizabeth positively liked parliament. Perhaps the best way of describing current views about her attitude is to say that she regarded parliament as a somewhat inconvenient necessity - with the emphasis on 'necessity'. It is clear that this necessity related to more than her need for parliamentary taxation. Elizabeth was very conservative. She valued existing ways of doing things and regarded most change with suspicion. Kings of England had traditionally sought the advice of their leading subjects on important issues as the need had arisen. Elizabeth had been brought up to believe that these attempts to establish a community of interest between the governor and the governed had played an important part in ensuring peace and stability in times past, and she was eager to see the tradition maintained. She was very aware that in the thirty years before her accession parliament had become firmly established as the forum in which this consultation took place, and she definitely had no intention of doing otherwise than accepting what she understood as having become 'custom and practice'. There is no doubt that the times when parliament was in session were periods of stress and strain for Elizabeth and that her irritation sometimes bubbled over into outbursts of ill-temper, but it is equally certain that she completely accepted that this was one of the many crosses which she was called upon to bear and that she was resigned to bearing it with the best grace that she could muster. In keeping with this view, it would be incorrect to judge the fine sentiments she expressed to parliament from time to time as being no more than cynical 'politician-speak'. Although it must be conceded that much of what was said was carefully contrived for effect rather than meaning - Elizabeth was a highly skilled and articulate political manipulator - there is every reason to believe that she was genuinely solicitous of her people's welfare, even if she portrayed herself as being much more altruistic than she really was.

6 Elizabeth's Dealings with Parliament

Constitutional historians use the phrases 'the queen-in-parliament' and 'the king-in-parliament' (depending on who was monarch at the time) to describe the highest authority in the land. This clumsy device has to be used because the reigning king or queen was in some ways a part of parliament and in some ways was not. For example, the monarch was not a member of either of the houses of parliament and was not allowed to attend their meetings in order to join in the debates. This was different to the practice in some other countries, such as Scotland, where the monarch was free to play a part in the day-to-day work of the representative assembly - a difference that was to give rise to some 'misunderstandings' when James VI of Scotland became James I of England in 1603. But in other ways Elizabeth, as queen, was very much a part of parliament. She could attend it in person in order to address the members of both Houses. These formal occasions took place at her request and were held in the House of Lords, with the members of the House of Commons standing uncomfortably in the confined space 'at the bar', the rail that separated the inner sanctum of the House of Lords from the area reserved for non-members who were called upon to attend a meeting of the upper house. Such personal appearances by Elizabeth in parliament were rare and were effectively confined to the opening and closing of each session. Her attendance at the closing of a session was particularly significant because it was here that she exercised her most overt parliamentary power - the granting or withholding of the royal assent to the bills that had passed both Houses. The granting of the royal assent was essential if a bill was to become law as an act of parliament. The word 'veto' is used to describe the withholding of the royal assent.

When historians first became aware that Elizabeth made extensive use of her veto it was assumed that this meant that she was on the political defensive, having to rely on a last ditch stand to prevent parliament from enacting legislation that was against her interests. However, a close scrutiny of the surviving evidence has proved that this is a misleading interpretation. It is possible to be sure about what happened in only the first half of the reign - the major records for the parliamentary sessions of 1584 to 1601 have been lost - but there is no reason to believe that there was a significant change in the way in which the veto was used as the queen grew older. On average five bills were vetoed at the end of each of the first seven parliamentary sessions of the reign - hence the initial assumption that here was a feature of major political importance.

However, when the vetoed bills are examined it becomes clear that Elizabeth was not acting as dramatically as had been suspected. It seems safe to conclude that 8 of the 34 bills in question were rejected because of flaws in their drafting. At least, this appears to be the most reasonable explanation of the fact that all of the bills became law in a slightly amended form in subsequent sessions. Certainly, the poor drafting of bills was a major problem throughout the period and was the reason why dozens of them failed to make progress within parliament itself. Given this situation, it seems probable that the queen was advised to reject these bills because it was discovered at a late stage that faults in their wording were likely to result in unintended and undesirable consequences. Of the remaining vetoed bills, 21 did not impinge directly on any of the queen's interests. It seems that they were vetoed because, if they had become law, they were likely to have damaged the interests of individuals or groups whose points of view had not been considered when the bills had been discussed in parliament. There is no evidence to suggest that Elizabeth had anything to gain by vetoing these bills except protecting the public interest. That leaves just five occasions on which a bill was vetoed because the queen had a personal objection to its contents. Three of these were attempts to bring about changes in the Church of England that would move it in a more Protestant direction and two were directed against Mary, Queen of Scots, whom Elizabeth was for a long time determined to protect from punishment. Thus what at first sight appeared to be a heavy-handed use of the crown's power to veto turns out to be much lighter in touch.

This is not, of course, to suggest that Elizabeth in any sense kept her distance from events in parliament. Nor is there any reason to think that she would or should have. It is worth remembering that, although the past two centuries have conditioned us to expect a king or queen to play a purely ceremonial part in the life of parliament, the idea of a constitutional monarchy had not even been thought of when Elizabeth occupied the throne. Some Whig historians have given the impression that there was something vaguely improper in the fact that Elizabeth interfered in the workings of parliament. But such a view is anachronistic. In the sixteenth century very few people questioned the queen's right to influence parliament in whatever way she chose. Those who did take exception to any of the methods she used were looked upon with suspicion by most of their contemporaries. They were generally thought to be potentially dangerous disturbers of the public peace.

The most prominent of this small number of radicals were the MPs Peter and Paul Wentworth. On several occasions one or other of them got away with querying what was done in the queen's name, but when in 1576 Peter started a speech objecting to royal interference it was considered that he was going too far. The Speaker stopped him in mid-flow, he was arrested, and on the next day the Commons debated his case and decided to imprison him in the Tower of London. A hundred years later the supposed text of his speech was published. It was claimed to be taken from a contemporary record. The controversial section read:

1 Amongst other, Mr Speaker, two things do great hurt in this place, of which I do mean to speak: the one is a rumour which runneth about the House and this it is, "Take heed what you do, the queen's majesty liketh not such a matter. Whosoever prefereth it,
5 [puts it forward] she will be offended with him". Or on the contrary, "Her majesty liketh such a matter. Whosoever speaketh against it, she will be much offended with him". The other: sometimes a message is brought into the House, either of commanding or inhibiting, very injurious to the freedom of speech
10 and consultation. I would to God, Mr Speaker, that these two were buried in hell, I mean rumours and messages, for wicked undoubtedly they are. The reason is, the devil was first author of them, from whom proceedeth nothing but wickedness.

Of the two techniques complained of, the use of whispered rumours is the most difficult for the historian to assess. It is impossible either to quantify its use - although the impression given by the writings of the time is that it was commonplace - or to be sure whether the rumours originated from the queen herself, from one of her ministers, or even (unlikely as it might be) from a non-governmental source. Nor can the effect of the use of this technique be assessed with any degree of confidence. Because there is no direct evidence available, any commentator has to fall back on 'hunch' and 'feel'. All that can be said about such judgements is that they are or are not convincing, and that they are the best that can be managed in the circumstances. Here is a situation in which the opinion of a well informed student is likely to be as valid as those that appear in print. Each reader will be able to form a judgement about whether the use of such a technique was likely to have the desired effect.

The use of 'messages' was a much more straightforward matter. These were normally 'official' in that they were usually relayed openly and explicitly by a member of the Privy Council. It is not possible to be precise about the frequency with which this method of control was employed because no systematic record was kept of its use, but it is clear that it was a common occurrence. As Wentworth suggested, it could take the form of either an instruction that something be done or that it be ceased. Nobody has pulled together all the evidence about royal messages, but it is clear that most of the interventions were direct and unambiguous, with no room being left for MPs to ignore them without challenging the queen's authority. And such was the deference shown by nearly all MPs towards their prince that hardly a murmur was heard when, for instance, the House was told to end its discussion of religious reform or the succession, or was instructed to give priority to the consideration of public (rather than private) bills. The Commons could become very unco-operative, even spiteful, when it was widely felt that its dignity had been affronted (normally when the offence had been committed by the House of Lords or by an 'outsider'), but nearly all MPs seem to have accepted that it was the queen's right to tell them what to do and that her instructions were to be obeyed.

However, in practice, there were different 'levels' of control exercised by Elizabeth over parliamentary business. She was very specific and very directive where she felt that she needed to be but her interventions could be very low key at other times. In an age before the invention of the typewriter and the photocopier, when a bill was introduced into parliament it only existed in the form of a single handwritten copy - hence the term the 'first reading' of a bill was literally meant - and one way of indicating the queen's support for a measure was for her sign-manual (signature) to appear on the bill itself. It seems that this was generally taken to be a low-level intervention that could be ignored if there was good reason to do so. Perhaps promoters of legislation were able to secure this cachet of royal support by paying a set fee, and perhaps it was known that Elizabeth's personal involvement in a bill that carried the sign-manual was sometimes non-existent. This might explain why a bill with royal support was sometimes amended, was sometimes lost in the mass of unfinished business at the end of a session, and, on at least one occasion, failed to receive the royal assent even though it had been accepted by both Houses!

It is probably safe to assume that the use of the sign-manual did not ensure a bill's virtually automatic safe passage through both houses of parliament because the queen was content that it should not. There is no doubt that she could have forced the issue successfully had she felt strongly about the matter. However, there was one aspect of parliamentary management over which she was unable to get her way. Try as she would, Elizabeth could not brow-beat the House of Commons into arranging its affairs so as to make certain that all the legislation that the government proposed passed through the necessary stages to gain approval within the time-scale envisaged for the duration of parliament. Time after time instructions were given that the queen's business should take precedence over all else but, although each admonition appears to have yielded immediate results, the effect seems to have been short-lived. It was not that MPs were being obstructive. Part of the problem was that many of the members who were prepared to attend sittings of the House beyond the first few weeks of any session (attendance records were not kept, but it seems that up to three-quarters of MPs were absent during the second half of most sessions) were doing so primarily in order to pursue legislation in which they had a vested interest. They naturally attempted to ensure that the bills with which they were involved were given the required amount of parliamentary time. This was a particularly pressing need because there were always far more bills in the pipeline than could possibly emerge successfully as acts.

The other part of the problem which caused Elizabeth and her ministers so much frustration was that parliamentary procedures and administrative arrangements were such that they were bound to be overwhelmed by the deluge of draft legislation with which they had to cope. Perhaps there is no better illustration of the differences in thought processes between our modern problem-solving culture and the custom-based culture of sixteenth century England than the way in which Elizabeth and her ministers approached the issue of the parliamentary log-jam. Whereas it would appear self-evident to us that a solution would only be found if far-reaching changes were introduced, the queen (in common with all those around her) assumed that the answer must be to make existing systems function properly. Although it is an over-simplification, it is helpful to think of Elizabethans looking backwards for the solutions to their problems, as opposed to present-day governments which tend to look forwards.

Over the centuries the best known aspect of Elizabeth's dealings with parliament has been her making of speeches to the assembled members. Because these occasions were well documented - sometimes the royal printer was instructed to publish the text of what was said, presumably for national distribution - evidence about them has been one of the sources most readily available to those writing about the politics of the reign. Most of them make impressive reading. They are redolent of graciously condescending superiority and of a monarch whose first and last concerns were the welfare of her subjects. They are the stuff of historical romance, with the accounts written by members of the queen's audience including descriptions of MPs on bended knee listening in rapture to the honeyed phrases and sometimes being reduced to tears of joy by what they heard. It is therefore little wonder that nearly all historians have uncritically accepted the traditional view that Elizabeth is to be seen at her politically most skilful on such occasions. Nineteenth and early twentieth-century writers tended to use the speeches as evidence of the close relationship, based on mutual love and respect, that existed between Elizabeth and the people of England. They often contrasted this with the sourness that pervaded the reigns of the early Stuarts. In the era of the Neale orthodoxy the praise lavished on Elizabeth for her performances was almost as fulsome. Of course, the speeches were seen as fulfilling different purposes to those traditionally portrayed. Instead of being presented as the high points in an almost perfect love affair between ruler and ruled, they were characterised as the political master-strokes of a temporarily cornered monarch who needed to defuse dangerous situations that had been created by a vociferous parliamentary opposition. Revisionists historians have tended to accept the general 'feel' of the Neale line, but they have toned it down considerably. This has been necessary because it has been argued that when the speeches were made the queen was not in nearly such severe political difficulties as Neale claimed, and was therefore not under the degree of stress that would have made her performances especially admirable. It has also been pointed out that, contrary to the impression normally given, Elizabeth was not uniformly effective when she addressed parliament. In particular, attention has been drawn to her closing speech of 1566 when her contempt for those who had attempted to bring pressure to bear on her was very apparent. There certainly was no skilful pouring of oil on troubled waters here. However, even those who feel least at ease with traditional interpretations are content to accept in general terms that Elizabeth's speeches to parliament were something special.

The most famous of the addresses was delivered in 1601 and is known as the 'Golden Speech'. It was first so-named during the period when Elizabeth's record of parliamentary oratory was enthusiastically and uncritically acclaimed. This, the last of the queen's speeches to parliament, delivered when she was in her late sixties, was seen to be a fitting climax to a glorious reign. Although modern writers would not present it in the same light, they would agree that it is a prime example of many of the techniques used by Elizabeth in her dealings with parliament.

In the early part of the speech the well-worn theme of the love of her subjects being her most valuable possession was developed. Over and over again, from the time she was a young woman onwards, Elizabeth had shown that she fully appreciated how effective it was for a superior to show how much the goodwill of inferiors was valued. She had learned early in life that flattery delivered with a modicum of aloofness created feelings of affection and loyalty in the recipients, and it became one of her stock-in-trade techniques for overcoming discontent among any group with which she had dealings. Of a similar nature was the next theme to be introduced. This was the queen's portrayal of herself as an altruist, all of whose decisions were guided by what she thought would be good for her people. Her message was that she was above such plebeian considerations as self-interest.

1 Of myself I must say this: I never was any greedy, scraping grasper, nor a straight fast-holding Prince, nor yet a waster. My heart was never set on any worldly goods, but only for my subjects' good. What you bestow on me, I will not hoard it up, but receive it to
5 bestow on you again.

She then moved on to the subject of monopolies. This was the issue that had aroused a great deal of anger and ill-feeling in the Commons during the session, especially as serious discontent on the same topic had been headed-off in the previous parliamentary session (1597) by fine words from the queen which had resulted in no action.

1 Since I was queen, yet did I never put my pen to any grant but that, upon pretext and semblance made unto me, it was both good and beneficial to the subjects in general, though a private profit to some of my ancient servants who had deserved well at my hands ... If my
5 kingly bounties have been abused, and my grants turned to the hurt of my people, contrary to my will and meaning, and if any authority under me have neglected or perverted what I have committed to them, I hope God will not lay their culps and offences to my charge; who, though there were danger in repealing
10 our grants, yet what danger would I not rather incur for your good, than would I suffer them to continue?

The techniques used by Elizabeth to deflect blame from herself were those used by most of the politically adroit monarchs of the modern age. The fact that they were only effective where a basic trust existed between prince and people, coupled with the clear evidence that the speech was very well received indeed is an indication that even at the end of her reign Elizabeth was still held in high esteem by the political nation as a whole. In no small part this was the result of the way in which she had dealt with parliament over a period of more than 40 years.

Making notes on 'Elizabeth and Parliament'

As far as note making is concerned it is helpful to think of the chapter as being made up of three distinct parts. The first part (section 1) is designed to alert you to differences between the modern and the Elizabethan parliamentary systems. The understandings you have gained from reading it should be all you need. It is probably unnecessary to make any notes on this part of the chapter. The second part (sections 2, 3, & 4) explores the historiographical dimension of the subject, centring on the Neale interpretation. This forms a popular and self-contained examination topic and is worth noting in detail. Your aim should be to compile a set of notes from which you will be able to write an entire essay. The third part (sections 5 & 6) examines the relationship between Elizabeth and parliament. This material needs to be placed alongside all the other evidence you will use to form conclusions about the queen's performance as a ruler. You will already have gathered an amount of this (from chapters 2 & 4) and there will be more to come (from chapters 6 & 7). The notes you make from this part of the chapter, preferably on a separate sheet of paper, should concentrate on the issues about Elizabeth that you have already identified.

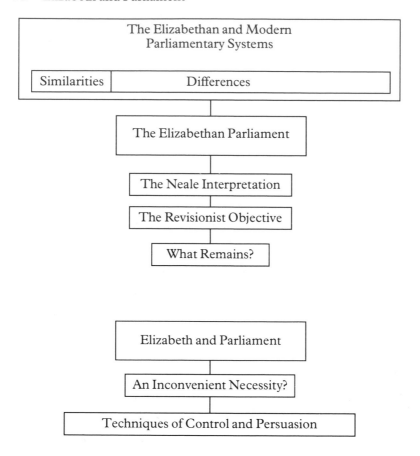

Summary - Elizabeth and Parliament

Answering essay questions on 'Elizabeth and Parliament'

Because of the dramatic way in which the Neale interpretation of Elizabethan parliamentary history has been modified by the work of revisionist historians, this topic has become a popular one among examiners. It should therefore be high on any priority list of issues to be included in a final revision schedule.

Although the questions that appear on examination papers rarely make explicit mention of the historiographical dimension of the topic, this is the aspect of the issue which normally lies at the heart of the essay titles. Study the following examples and check that this is so.

1   'The keynote of relations between Elizabeth I and parliament was co-operation not conflict.' Discuss.

2   How far is it accurate to claim that it was only Elizabeth I's skill in handling parliament that prevented there being a breakdown in trust between the queen and her people?

3   Why was so much discontent expressed in the parliaments of Elizabeth I's reign?

4   To what extent was parliament a 'necessary evil' in Elizabethan England?

These are all demanding titles, but they should not be too difficult to 'unlock' if a sound technique of question analysis is used. Look at question 4. The phrase which needs to be 'unpacked' stands out clearly. What is it? It is important to identify this and to do the unpacking, but in this case it is not the most important part of the analysis. The key to unlocking the question is spotting that the idea of parliament being a 'necessary evil' has no meaning unless words such as 'to whom?' or 'in whose opinion?' are added. Once this has been done, and as long as the need to reflect the historical debate is remembered, a range of suitable plans for the essay readily spring to mind. For example, there might be a two-part plan (the old orthodox interpretation and the revisionist interpretation), with the individuals or groups identified by asking the question 'to whom?' included in each part. What other plans would be appropriate?

Source-based questions on 'Elizabeth and Parliament'

1 Peter Wentworth on Parliamentary Liberties, 1576
Carefully read the extract from Peter Wentworth's speech, given on page 89. Answer the following questions.
a)   What two things is Wentworth complaining about? (2 marks)
b)   What reasons does he give for objecting to them? (3 marks)
c)   What, is it reasonable to surmise, were his real reasons for objecting? (3 marks)
d)   What significance was ascribed to this speech by J.E. Neale? (2 marks)

2 Elizabeth's Golden Speech, 1601
Carefully read the two extracts from Elizabeth's Golden Speech given on pages 92-3. Answer the following questions.
a)   In the first extract what three things does Elizabeth deny being? (3 marks)
b)   In the second extract who does Elizabeth blame for the creation of unpopular monopolies? (2 marks)
c)   Comment on the explanation that Elizabeth gives in both extracts of her intentions. (5 marks)
d)   What are the strengths and weaknesses of these extracts as evidence of Elizabeth's policy on the issue of monopolies? (5 marks)

CHAPTER 6

Elizabeth I, Marriage and the Succession

1 Background to the Marriage Issue

It has often been said that the most important thing about Elizabeth I was that she was female. Certainly this was a major issue to many of her contemporaries. There was virtually universal and unthinking acceptance of the prevailing attitudes about gender in sixteenth-century England. In a society which assumed that there was a divinely ordained order of things known as 'the chain of being', the place of women in the structure was thought to be clear-cut. At the top of the earthly hierarchy (there was also a heavenly one) were men. Below them were their dependants - women and children - who owed them honour and obedience. In return for their subservience these 'weaker beings' received food, clothing, shelter and protection. The 'natural' unit of society was thought to be the nuclear family of husband, wife and children, with servants if appropriate. Anybody who did not belong to one of these units was regarded with suspicion as a potentially disruptive influence. Thus the only acceptable roles for adult females were as wives or servants. Although it was taken for granted that at any one moment there would be a considerable number of unmarried women, it was assumed that these were effectively wives-in-waiting. As Elizabeth herself is reported as saying, 'There is a strong idea in the world that a woman cannot live unless she is married or at all events if she refrains from marriage she does so for some bad reason'.

It was believed that this fixed hierarchy related to 'position in society' as well as to age and sex. At the top of the chain was God. He appointed rulers over the various parts of the earth. Below the rulers (often referred to by the group name of 'princes') were the various orders of the ruled, ranging from nobles to servants, with the male head of each household imparting his status to his wife and children. The assumption running throughout was that females were inferiors who needed to be under male tutelage if they were to function effectively. The very idea of a woman ruler was therefore regarded by many people as an aberration which was contrary to the natural order of things. This point of view was most famously voiced by John Knox, the leading Scottish Protestant reformer, who fulminated against 'the monstrous regiment [rule] of women' in a pamphlet published in 1558. The words had been written with the two Marys - Mary Tudor, Queen of England and Mary of Guise, the Scottish regent - in mind. By chance, Mary Tudor died while the work was being printed, and on its appearance it was mistakenly thought to be an attack on Elizabeth's position as monarch in England. A hasty disclaimer headed off a potentially dangerous diplomatic crisis, but the fact remained that Knox had pinpointed a widely held discomfort with the idea of a female ruler.

In England this discomfort was rarely translated into active opposition. This was because an equally strongly-held belief about the rights of inheritance pointed in an opposite direction. Perhaps it was a relatively early manifestation of the famed British sense of fair play, based on a belief in natural justice, but the population as a whole was strongly attached to the notion that links of blood should determine the passage of power and property (including the position of ruler) from person to person. It was felt that this was the will of God, which man had no right to set aside. The strength of this sentiment is illustrated by the way in which its operation was supported even when to do so was at best inconvenient. The clearest example of this phenomenon occurred when Edward VI died in 1553. The most powerful man in the country, the Duke of Northumberland, attempted to place Lady Jane Grey, a descendant of Henry VIII's younger sister, on the throne. Edward's 'natural' successor - as he had no children or brothers - was his elder sister, Mary. She was a committed Catholic whereas Jane Grey was a Protestant who could be expected to support the religious changes that had been made since Henry's death in 1547. Nevertheless, many Protestants supported Mary's claim over that of Jane Grey, even though the result was likely to be their own eventual persecution. They seem to have believed that God had willed a female Catholic ruler on the country as a sign of his displeasure!

It is therefore not surprising that Elizabeth, being Henry VIII's only surviving child, was almost universally accepted as Mary's successor in 1558. There was considerable apprehension caused by the fact that she was a woman, but it was understood that this was a difficulty that would have to be lived with as there was no way in which it could be overcome. It was generally assumed that as Elizabeth was single, yet still of marriageable age (she was 25), the problem of her gender would largely be overcome by finding her a suitable husband. This would have the double advantage of placing her under male authority (with her consort ruling jointly with her as king but presumably playing the leading role), and of hopefully providing heirs to the throne in due course. The main difficulty would be in deciding who should be her husband. Potential partners fell into two categories - Englishmen and foreigners. Both groups had inherent drawbacks. An Englishman would, by definition, be of non-royal stock as there were no surviving male relatives of the House of Tudor of marriageable age. In addition, there were likely to be considerable problems caused by effectively raising a native noble family to royal status. The resulting social rivalry had often been destructive when a king had taken an English bride: how much more would it be the case were an Englishman to become king-consort. Had there been a pre-eminent noble family with a candidate who was suitable by age and aptitude the problem might have been containable, but this was not the case.

On the surface, the possibility of finding a foreign husband for Elizabeth seemed to be less fraught with difficulties. Such a solution to the marriage problem would avoid upsetting the power balance within the English nobility and should not bring in its train cohorts of greedy relatives all wishing to gain from their family's good fortune. However, a foreign match might result in a different set of potentially disastrous consequences. In particular, England might become no more than a satellite of the bridegroom's domains, with its interests being sacrificed to those of the new king's territories. This possibility was at the forefront of the minds of most members of England's political elite in 1558. It was generally believed that this is what had happened after Mary had married Philip II of Spain, leading to the loss of Calais, England's last continental outpost. There was a widespread determination that a similar situation should not be allowed to arise again in the future.

A separate, but still important, issue was the religious affiliation of any potential husband, be he English or foreign. It was assumed that, whatever Elizabeth's views might be, the country would end up following the confessional stance of its new king. This was certain to be divisive. If the favoured candidate were to be a Catholic, the Protestants - especially those with whom Elizabeth surrounded herself - would face a bleak political and religious future. If a Protestant were to be chosen, Catholics and those of conservative religious views would face the prospect of a religious lurch to the left and would lose all hope of an eventual triumph for their cause now that there was likely to be a Protestant heir to the throne. Once, in 1559, it became clear that the queen's religious stance was to be moderate Protestant, but with freedom of conscience guaranteed to all believers, it seemed likely that any marriage would upset the delicate balance over religion that had been struck. This meant that, although those who were strongly committed to either confession were eager to promote a match with a candidate of their own persuasion, those whose prime concern was the political stability of the country became increasingly concerned that any marriage would prove to be disruptive, especially in religious affairs.

2 Early Possibilities of Marriage

It might seem surprising that when Elizabeth came to the throne she was still unmarried although she was in her twenty-sixth year. Certainly it was very unusual for the daughter of a king to remain unwed into her twenties. The norm was for girls of royal parentage to be 'spent' in the dynastic marriage market while they were still in their teens. Henry VIII's daughters were exceptions to the rule because of the uncertainties that surrounded their status during the prime years of their 'marketability'. Both Mary and Elizabeth were declared bastards by their father when his marriages to their mothers were nullified, which meant at the very least that their royalty was tainted. Then, towards the end of Henry's life, when they were recognised as second and third in line of succession, they became too valuable to be married off while their brother was too young to have children. They needed to be kept in reserve, which was increasingly the case with Elizabeth once her brother's ill-health presaged an early death, and then her sister's age made motherhood a receding possibility for her. Hence a husband had yet to be found for the queen who ascended the throne in November 1558.

There was certainly no shortage of volunteers. The first to let it be known that he would be pleased to raise Elizabeth from her unmarried status was Philip II of Spain. He expected that his dead wife's sister would be grateful to be made such an offer which would ensure the continuity and stability of the political régime in England. From Philip's point of view, it would also ensure that Spain and England would continue to work together in the struggle with France, as well as earning him the credit for having kept England in the Catholic fold. However, the ex-King-Consort of England was not slow to recognise Elizabeth's evasiveness when discussing the proposal with his ambassador for what it was, a stalling tactic intended to retain Spanish friendship for as long as possible but with no intention of ever agreeing to a match. Philip was therefore quick both to make other marriage plans for himself and to suggest other candidates for Elizabeth's hand. The names advanced were those of two of his cousins, the Austrian Habsburg archdukes Ferdinand and Charles, who were younger sons of the Holy Roman Emperor.

Elizabeth was prepared to consider both men because it was politic to do so, Philip having recommended them. However, it was quickly decided that Ferdinand would not be suitable: he was well known for his aggressively Catholic stance on religious matters. But, as the possibility of a match with Charles remained, the decision to proceed no further with Ferdinand caused no great offence. Because Charles was thought to be more flexible over religion and because Elizabeth wished to retain Habsburg good will, soundings-out about the archduke continued, on and off, for nearly a decade, although in retrospect it is clear that there was never any serious intent on Elizabeth's part. She and her advisers were merely playing a diplomatic game. Their hope was to ensure the continued friendship of the Habsburgs towards England without having to pay a price for it.

There were other foreign princes besides the Habsburgs who sought the queen's hand in marriage. One, in particular, made quite an impact, although for the wrong reasons. Prince Eric, the heir to the Swedish throne, had first been offered to Elizabeth as a husband during Mary's reign, but his suit had been rejected. Once Elizabeth ascended the throne an ambassador was sent by the King of Sweden to renew the offer. This time the Swedes were taken advantage of unmercifully. They were given encouragement in the vaguest of terms, along with broad hints that their cause would be helped by the distribution of expensive gifts to the queen and her leading courtiers. Several 'rounds' of costly presents were extracted from the gullible Scandinavians who, unknowingly, were thereby making themselves the focus of ridicule throughout the court and the capital. The farce reached its height when Eric's brother, accompanied by a large retinue of nobles, arrived in London to woo on his brother's behalf. Once again largesse was scattered far and wide, to the patronising amusement of the recipients of the misjudged generosity. In all it took about two years for the Swedes to realise that they were being made fools of. The episode illustrates the dangers of blindly attempting to influence decisions in a society where the ground rules are very different from one's own.

Throughout the first year of the new queen's reign London was awash with rumours about the likely identity of the man who would win Elizabeth as his bride. Despite the paucity of 'old' noble families and the general lack of eligible bachelors in those that did exist, one English peer was canvassed as a potentially suitable partner for Elizabeth. This was the Earl of Arundel. But there was little to commend him other than the fact that his family had possessed its earldom for twelve generations. He was middle-aged, Catholic, and dull. It was soon made clear to him that his advances were not welcomed. However, there was one Englishman who was thought to have a good chance of success. Sir William Pickering was of a similar age to the Earl of Arundel but there the similarity ceased. Pickering was a skilful courtier who knew how to make himself a pleasing companion. The fact that he was out of the country when Mary died and was prevented by sickness from returning for several months thereafter allowed plenty of time for speculation to mount before he actually presented himself at court. Throughout the summer of 1559 he spent several hours on most days in close contact with Elizabeth and it was widely expected that a marriage announcement was imminent. However, it seems that there was plenty of friendship but little romance and, in the absence of any 'political' gain to be made by the queen in plucking a husband from the ranks of the gentry, the relationship failed to make headway. In any case, it soon appeared that Elizabeth had found true love elsewhere.

3 Lord Robert Dudley (Earl of Leicester)

Robert Dudley was accorded the courtesy title of Lord because he was the son of a duke. Although his father, the Duke of Northumberland, had held a top-ranking peerage for only a few years, having been promoted in Edward VI's reign and having been executed at the end of it for attempting to place Lady Jane Grey on the throne, he had been able to ensure that all his many children benefited from his status. Lord Robert also inherited large helpings of ambition and self-confidence from his father.

For more than a century writers, especially of historical fiction, have been fascinated by the relationship between Dudley (created Earl of Leicester in 1564) and Elizabeth. The story is full of romance, mystery, intrigue, hope, and despair, stretching over more than thirty years. It is little wonder that multitudes of books and films have been based on the saga. The first chapter in the story lasted from late 1559 to early 1561. During this period the queen and her favourite seem to have been passionately in love with one another. The mutual physical attraction was strong and they clearly revelled in each other's company. In addition, two intertwining factors added drama to the situation. In September 1560 Dudley was widowed in strange circumstances, and in the following weeks Elizabeth was visibly torn between what she wanted to do and what she thought it was sensible to do. Lord Robert's wife, Amy Robsart, was found dead at the bottom of the stairs in a house from which all the servants had been sent away as being temporarily surplus to requirements. Although it was claimed that Amy had died naturally as the result of a fall, a widely circulating rumour had it that she had been murdered on Dudley's orders. It was even suggested that Elizabeth was a co-conspirator in the plot. Both Lord Robert and the queen vigorously proclaimed their innocence, but they seem generally not to have been believed. Historians have been divided on the issue ever since. While all admit that the evidence is not conclusive (no charges would stand up in a court of law), some have maintained that both 'lovers' were almost certainly guilty, and others have erected plausible explanations in support of the 'accident' theory. Speculation on the subject is interesting but in the end is unlikely to be productive. What, however, is of considerable historical significance is the way in which the rumours were fuelled, and the effects of the suspicions that lingered on.

Amy Robsart had been seriously ill, probably with cancer, for some time before her death. The story had circulated that she was being slowly poisoned by her husband who wished to be free to marry again. There is clear evidence that both this rumour and the persistent suggestion that when she died she was pushed rather than fell were encouraged by Sir William Cecil, who was doing all he could to discourage the queen from marrying Dudley. It could be argued that the Secretary was acting in what he considered to be Elizabeth's best interests - her reputation would have been irretrievably damaged had a marriage gone ahead in such circumstances - but it has to be admitted that Cecil had everything to lose had Dudley become king, when presumably his services would have been dispensed with. Certainly, he seems to have been beside himself with a mixture of rage and anxiety for several weeks in the autumn of 1560 when it seemed that Elizabeth was determined to go ahead despite all the adverse publicity. In the end, however, the queen's sense of what was politically possible triumphed over her personal inclinations (often portrayed as a victory of head over heart), and she decided that Dudley must remain a friend rather than becoming a spouse. But her resolve was hard won and even then weakened from time to time when she allowed herself to hope that the impossible might indeed be possible. Signs of the anguish caused by the dilemma she faced were evident in her behaviour well into 1561. It is conceivable that, had Cecil not worked so hard to reinforce public doubts about Dudley, Elizabeth might have taken the risk of marrying the man she loved. But, of course, we can never know for certain.

4 Background to the Succession Issue

In October 1562 Elizabeth almost died of smallpox. The news caused a deep sense of foreboding to spread among many members of the political classes. The spectre of serious civil strife, and even of civil war, raised its head. The problem was that it was not clear who would succeed Elizabeth were she to die without children. There were no more descendants of Henry VIII, which meant that it would be necessary to look to those whose Tudor blood came from one of Henry's two sisters to find the next English monarch (see the genealogical table on page 103). Had one of the first line (coming from a first child-bearing marriage) of these been an adult male the situation might not have been so fraught, but all of Margaret and Mary's surviving first-line descendants were female. The obvious successor based on precedence of birth was Margaret Tudor's grand-daughter, Mary, Queen of Scots.

Unfortunately Mary was a most controversial candidate. Due to the death of her father she had become the reigning Queen of Scotland when she was a young baby. While still a child she had been sent to France to be brought up by her mother's relations, the powerful Guise family, in preparation for her marriage to the Dauphin, the heir to the French throne. When the Dauphin had become king as Francis II in 1559 the kingdoms of husband and wife had been declared combined as one political entity. A claim had also been made to the English throne in Mary's name, it being argued that Henry VIII and Anne Boleyn had never legally been married and that therefore Elizabeth had no right to be Queen of England. Although no action - apart from incorporating the English lions in the couple's coat of arms - had been taken to make good Mary's claim, and although by 1562 Francis had died, the union between France and Scotland had been dissolved, and Mary was no longer Queen of France, the suspicion of the Queen of Scots was as widespread in England as it had ever been. This was considerable and of long-standing. It had begun in the early-1540s after Henry VIII had failed to force the Scots to agree to a marriage between Mary and his son Edward, and it had resulted in parliament passing legislation to debar Margaret Tudor's descendants from succeeding to the English throne. At the time when Elizabeth's life was threatened by smallpox the most common concern about Mary was that she was thought to be a French

The Succession to Elizabeth I

Elizabeth was the last of the Tudors on the male line. Her closest relatives on her father's side were the descendants of her two aunts, Margaret (the elder) and Mary (the younger). As Elizabeth's reign progressed a series of deaths simplified the issue of the succession. By 1578 all the legally recognised descendants of Mary Tudor (her younger aunt) were dead, as were all but one of Margaret Tudor's descendants by 1587. This left just James VI of Scotland with a claim to be a legitimate successor to Elizabeth.

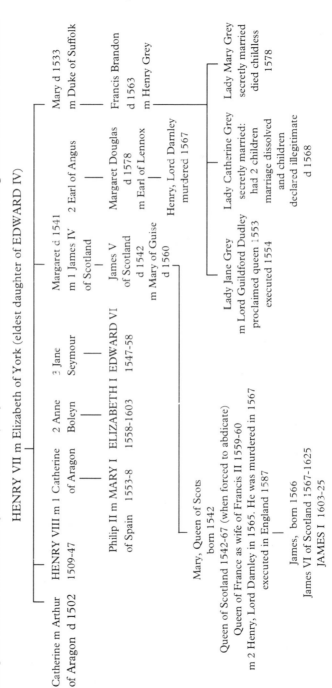

HENRY VII m Elizabeth of York (eldest daughter of EDWARD IV)

pawn. It was feared that were she to inherit the English crown her new kingdom would become a satellite of France in the same way that Scotland had become. In addition, those who felt committed to the Protestant church settlement that had taken place under Elizabeth disliked the fact that Mary was a Catholic who was unlikely to accept the religious *status quo* in England.

The arrangement for the succession made by Henry VIII had been for the grand-daughters of his sister Mary to be next in line after his own children. The eldest of these, Lady Jane Grey, had subsequently been executed because she was the object of the Duke of Northumberland's unsuccessful *coup* in 1553. This left Jane's two sisters, Lady Catherine Grey and Lady Mary Grey, as potential 'blockers' to the Queen of Scots' candidature. However, both were young women of no great personality who aroused little enthusiasm even among their supporters. So some of those who were strongly opposed to the prospect of Mary, Queen of Scots, becoming Queen of England looked around for other possible contenders to the throne. Their options were very limited because there were few people with even a distant blood relationship with English royalty from the past. There were a couple of descendants of Margaret Tudor via her second marriage with the Scottish nobleman the Earl of Angus, and there was one rather unconvincing claimant, the Earl of Huntington, who had an amount of pre-Tudor royal blood in his veins. But those who championed either of these causes were desperate indeed. The unwelcome truth was that there was little alternative to the Queen of Scotland were Elizabeth to die before she could provide an heir of her own body.

5 The Campaign over the Succession

For most property owners in England worrying about the succession was almost a way of life. Certainly, it was something they were very used to. Almost for as long as anyone could remember there had been public concern about the political future of the country. During the middle part of Henry VIII's reign there had been disquiet over his inability to sire a male heir. This had been followed by doubts over the health of his son, once he had one, allied to the knowledge that in any case Henry was unlikely to live long enough for Edward to reach maturity before he became king - thus necessitating a regency or protectorate régime which past experience suggested would at best be weak and divisive. Then there was the prospect of Edward dying before he could father any children, thereby bringing a female to the throne for effectively the first time in English history. It was assumed that this would usher in a period of weak government and further uncertainty about the future, the more so because it was thought likely that Mary would be too old to bear children. Although the death of Mary and the accession of Elizabeth were welcomed as heralding a new dawn, there was a widespread hope that the new queen would secure the succession as speedily as possible by marrying and producing children. This desire was strongly expressed as early as the first parliament of the reign.

By the time parliament met for the second time in 1563 the questions of the queen's marriage and the succession were at the top of many MPs' agendas. The undoubted strength of feeling that already existed was orchestrated by members of the Privy Council in an attempt to pressurise Elizabeth into taking action, especially over the issue of the succession. The hope seems to have been to secure an explicit decision, encapsulated in legislation, about the order in which the possible claimants to the throne were to succeed Elizabeth should the situation arise. The intention of many was to find a way of eliminating Mary, Queen of Scots, as a possible successor. However, the Councillors' ploy did not work on this occasion. When her attempts to warn the two houses of parliament off the subject were ignored, Elizabeth met the situation head on. She summoned a deputation of both houses to her and informed them of her intentions. She is reported as having said:

1 Therefore I will answer give. The two petitions that you presented me in many words expressed, contained these two things in sum as of your cares the greatest: my marriage and my successor. Of which two the last I think is best to be touched, and of the other a silent
5 thought may serve; for I had thought it had been so desired as none other tree's blossoms should have been minded or hope of my fruit had been denied you. And by the way, if any here doubt that I am as it were by vow or determination bent never to trade that life, put out that heresy; your belief is awry; for as I think it best for a private
10 woman, so do I strive with myself to think it not meet for a prince. And if I can bend my will to your need I will not resist such a mind. But to the last, think not that you had needed this desire if I had seen a time so ripe to be denounced. The greatness of the cause therefore and need of your returns, doth make me say that which I
15 think the wise may easily guess: that as a short time for so long a continuance ought not to pass by rote, as many telleth tales, even so, as cause by conference with the learned shall the matter worthy utterance for your behoofs, so shall I more gladly pursue your good after my days than with my prayers be a means to linger my living
20 thread. And this much more than I had thought will I add for your comfort; I have good record in this place that other means than you mentioned have been thought of, perchance for your good as much as for my surety no less, which if presently could conveniently have been executed, had not been deferred. But I hope I shall die in
25 quiet with *nunc dimittis,* which cannot be without I see some glimpse of your following surety after my graved bones.

This convoluted statement seems to have been understood by those who heard it, although Elizabeth appears to have attempted to obscure her meaning more than to clarify it. In fact, the address is a prime example of the queen's ability to speak many words but to say very little when she wished to be evasive. Yet the communication was well enough received. Perhaps this was because many members of parliament recognised in the tone of the speech - it had to be this as it contained little exact meaning - Elizabeth's intention to act in both matters (marriage and the succession) with the best interests of her people in mind. The fact that the royal statement did not provoke a collective response of dissatisfaction suggests both that Elizabeth was greatly trusted (and feared?) and that the more politically aware realised that they had taken the matter about as far as they could for the moment.

When parliament next met in 1566 many MPs were clearly perturbed that the queen had neither married nor named a successor. Once again there was considerable agitation aimed at persuading Elizabeth to take some definite action. But the queen was not to be moved. Her response, read on her behalf at the closing ceremony, was clearer than it had been three years earlier, but it was dismissive in tone (lacking her normal skill in making an audience feel good) and openly challenging in content. Parliament was told that both issues were the queen's business and that she would take action when the time was right. As the years passed by it became clear to increasing numbers of people that as far as the succession was concerned the time would never be right.

In 1565 Mary, Queen of Scots, had married for a second time. Her choice of husband appeared to be a happy blend of personal inclination and political shrewdness. The man chosen to be the new King of Scotland was Henry, Lord Darnley, towards whom Mary felt a powerful physical attraction. In addition, he was the only surviving male descendant of the Tudor line - albeit via Margaret Tudor's second marriage, and thus of inferior status - and therefore conferred on any children that Mary might bear him a virtually unstoppable claim to the English throne should Elizabeth die without issue.

Elizabeth was furious when she found out about the marriage, which had taken place against her express wishes. For several years she had been scheming to persuade Mary to select a husband who was clearly pro-English. Although the evidence is not conclusive - as was becoming the norm, Elizabeth did not consistently make her intentions clear - it seems that she wanted Mary to chose Robert Dudley as her spouse. She had created him Earl of Leicester in 1564 to overcome Mary's objection that he was not a 'proper' noble, and appears to have been prepared to recognise any offspring of the union as first in line to the English succession as her part of the bargain. If, as seems virtually certain, Elizabeth was serious in pressing for the Dudley match, she handled matters very badly. The manoeuvres she engaged in were ponderous and obscure, and she never faced up to the fact that Mary's pride would not allow her to accept as her husband the man who was widely thought to be the Queen of England's cast-off lover. She had virtually dared Mary to assert her independence, and was not a little displeased when the challenge was taken up in style.

Elizabeth's anger was almost unconfined when a year after the marriage Mary gave birth to a healthy son, whom she named James. It seemed that in effect Mary had gained all that Elizabeth had ever been prepared to offer her without having to pay a political price for it. The Queen of England had been comprehensively outmanoeuvred. But then Mary proceeded to throw away her winning hand. She made one disastrous decision after another. Having come to loath her husband, who admittedly treated her in a boorish and petulant manner, she not only formed an illicit liaison with one of her subjects, the Earl of Bothwell, but conspired with him to murder her uncongenial spouse. Despite the facts that Bothwell's guilt was widely known and that her own complicity was generally suspected, Mary rushed into marriage with her dead husband's murderer. This was too much for her powerful Protestant nobles to bear. They rose up in rebellion, defeated Bothwell's forces, captured Mary, and forced her to abdicate in favour of her infant son.

In 1568 the Queen of Scots escaped from captivity, fled to England, and called upon Elizabeth to render her assistance in recovering her throne. For the next twenty years - the full story is told in John Warren's companion volume in this series - the two queens played an ever more bizarre game of pretence and make-believe. Mary became increasingly desperate as her captivity showed no sign of ending. She explicitly involved herself in plots whose clear purpose was to assassinate Elizabeth and to install herself as Queen of England. For her part, Elizabeth drove her ministers nearly to distraction by refusing to take action against somebody whom she insisted on regarding as a fellow monarch, despite the facts that her subjects had deposed her, that she was a prisoner completely in England's power, and that her activities were having a destabilising effect on English politics. In the end, in 1587, the issue was only resolved by Elizabeth being tricked by her ministers into agreeing to Mary's execution on charges of treason.

So, for virtually the first three decades of Elizabeth's reign, Mary, Queen of Scots, was the *de facto*, although unrecognised, heir to the English throne. Despite the concerted efforts of large sections of the (Protestant) political classes to manoeuvre Elizabeth into disbaring Mary from the succession, either directly or indirectly by a subterfuge such as placing the choice of a successor in the hands of a parliament to be summoned immediately the current monarch died, no official pronouncement about the succession was ever made. As a consequence, the issue remained one of the most controversial political topics between 1558 and 1587. However, the subject thereafter lost its power to disconcert ministers and to divide political opinion. With Mary dead, there was no longer the fear of there being a future monarch who was both a Catholic and the pawn of one of the major continental powers (during the last 15 years of her life Mary had been thought of as a creature of the King of Spain, from whom she hoped to receive military support for her various planned *coups*, rather than of the King of France, as had earlier been the case). It was tacitly agreed that Mary's son, James VI of Scotland, would become the next king of England on Elizabeth's death. This was not a frightening prospect. James was known to be a sound Protestant of moderate views and he was not under the influence of, nor owed obligations to, either France or Spain. He was universally regarded as a 'safe' candidate, and by 1603 it was accepted throughout the country that he would be England's next monarch. Therefore, when Elizabeth died, James journeyed south from Edinburgh secure in the knowledge that his claim to the throne was totally uncontested.

6 Elizabeth's Behaviour over the Succession

In recent decades the weight of historical opinion has been that Elizabeth behaved badly over the question of the succession. She has been criticised for putting her own interests before those of her country. The case against her has normally been made in the following terms: Elizabeth feared that if her successor were named that person would act as a focal point, whatever were the wishes of the person concerned, for opposition to her rule. In such circumstances numbers of people, possibly including some of the most powerful men in the land, would feel that their first duty of loyalty was to the nominated successor rather than to Elizabeth herself. As a result, there would be a real likelihood of uprisings taking place in the interests of the successor, and Elizabeth's life would be seriously at risk. Because of these fears Elizabeth refused to allow a decision about her successor to be made, realising that while this was the case her most influential subjects would have a vested interest in keeping her alive so that the chaos that was likely to follow her death would be postponed for as long as possible. By so doing she was displaying the height of selfishness, sentencing the country to political turmoil and probable civil strife after her death (when she would no longer be affected by what happened), so that she could enjoy relative peace and quiet, and probable freedom from assassination attempts, during her lifetime.

Evidence to support this interpretation has not been difficult to find. On several occasions Elizabeth herself was reported as explaining her reluctance to name her successor in essentially these terms, although, of course, she presented her motives as being the national interest rather than her own. She even described how her experience of being the nominated heir during Mary's reign had convinced her that it was a public danger to have an acknowledged monarch-in-waiting. It has therefore seemed to some commentators that Elizabeth has effectively been condemned out of her own mouth. However, it seems very possible that a 'guilty' verdict has been handed down with insufficient scrutiny of all the facts. It is actually quite a simple matter to construct a plausible argument to support the contention that Elizabeth really was acting for the good of the country in one of those happy circumstances in which what was good for the leader was also good for the led.

At the heart of the argument is the contention that in the politics of Elizabethan England there was more to be gained by keeping the options open than there was by closing them down. This was an approach that the queen used to good effect in many aspects of public life. In religious matters she was careful not to drive her Catholic subjects and their conservative sympathisers into active opposition to her by forcing them to choose between abandoning their beliefs and engaging in rebellion. She left them the option of being both an adherent of the old faith and a loyal subject of the existing régime. She helped to make it possible for the pope to delay pronouncing her a heretic, and therefore deposed from her throne, until 1570 by preserving the impression that she might, at some stage, return her kingdom to obedience to Rome. In foreign affairs she kept alive the prospect of continued friendship with France and with Spain for longer than seemed reasonably possible in order to reduce the likelihood of offensive action being taken against her by them - separately or, worse still, in tandem. The same technique of ensuring that those with whom she had dealings were allowed to continue living in hope was routinely employed by Elizabeth in domestic politics. Seekers after patronage were normally kept dangling for what must have seemed an eternity. Even the greatest of favourites could be kept waiting for years before they gained the 'prizes' they had been promised and on which they had set their hearts. There is no doubt that Elizabeth understood that those who held hope for the future were more open to her influence than those who had already achieved their aspirations. She also fully appreciated that for each person satisfied by a decision there were likely to be several made discontented by having had hope removed from them.

This strategy of keeping options open in order to allow as many people as possible to continue living in hope may well have been the wisest one to adopt when dealing with the issue of the succession. If Elizabeth had given way to the persistent pressure exerted on her, especially in 1563 and 1566, but right up to 1587, to make legal arrangements for the succession, what would the effect have been? Assuming that the decision would have been to disallow Mary, Queen of Scots' claim to the throne, as had already happened towards the end of Henry VIII's reign, would political stability - the avowed aim of those who clamoured for a decision - have been increased? It seems unlikely that it would have been. Would most of those Catholics and their sympathisers who were able to justify remaining politically inactive while Elizabeth lived because there was the prospect of a Catholic succession have remained content to do nothing were Mary's claim to be overturned? Probably not. If Mary's son James had been declared heir-apparent would England's leading political figures have been able to resist the temptation of attempting to protect their futures by devoting much of their attention to building up their influence in Edinburgh? Would that have had a beneficial effect on English political life? It is hard to see that it would have. So where would have been the gain in taking legal action to remove uncertainties about the succession? The frustrations of those who wanted something to be done are understandable, but it does appear that they were seeking an impossible certainty. Perhaps Elizabeth was correct in her assessment that any attempt to tamper with the 'natural' succession would be doomed to failure. Certainly there is a case to be made that even had her 'do-nothing' policy not been blessed with good fortune - her own longevity, the death of Mary, Queen of Scots, and the survival of James - it would still have been the least bad of the options available to her. Just because it served her own self-interest and was opposed by the majority of her leading subjects, it does not mean that the approach was not the best one.

7 The French Match

In the years following her decision not to marry Lord Robert Dudley, which was made in the spring of 1562 at the latest, Elizabeth worked hard to convert her 'lover' into her 'best friend'. She made it clear to him that she loved him dearly, that no-one else was ahead of him in her affections, but that there could be no question of them being anything more than very good friends. Thereafter the relationship was close and enduring, even if it was tempestuous at times. When serious problems arose between them, as they did on at least half a dozen occasions, the cause was usually the same. Dudley (or Leicester as he became in 1564, and as he will be referred to from here on) presumed too much on his sovereign's friendship and acted in a manner that a proud queen could not accept from a subject. This situation was typified by Elizabeth's much quoted (and possibly apocryphal) outburst to Leicester in 1565 that 'God's death, my Lord, I will have here one mistress but no master'. But however much Leicester upset and offended the queen, sometimes leading to his banishment from court in disgrace, he was always reinstated in Elizabeth's good books once passions had cooled. There is little doubt that he was regarded by the queen as the one real love of her life - even if she lost sight of the fact from time to time - right up to the time of his death in 1588 and beyond. For his part, Leicester was much less committed. Self-interest seems to have been the driving force in the relationship as far as he was concerned. He used his position as royal favourite primarily to acquire for himself as much wealth, power, and status as possible. There is little evidence that he ever acted towards the queen with anything but selfishness as a motive. Cynics might argue that he was not to blame for this as he was merely being a typical man!

But, of course, the decision not to marry Leicester did not mean that Elizabeth was committed to remaining single. The possibility of her accepting some foreign prince as a consort was too good a diplomatic card not to be played. For much of the 1560s the Austrian Habsburg Archduke Charles remained the subject of marital speculation. However, in 1567 it became clear that every delaying tactic imaginable had been used and exhausted by the English side and it had to be admitted that the suit must now be allowed to lapse. However, other possibilities soon emerged. When Henry II of France had been killed in a tragic accident in 1559 he had left behind him an able and ambitious widow, Catherine de Medici, and four young sons. The eldest of these (Francis, the first husband of Mary, Queen of Scots) had succeeded him but had only lived for one year. The second had then became king as Charles IX. This had left two more princes of the blood, the Dukes of Anjou and Alençon, who could be used by Catherine de Medici in the export-marriage market. In 1570 she offered Anjou to Elizabeth as an indication of her good faith in the negotiations for an alliance she was conducting with England. The offer was treated with the seriousness that the situation warranted, but it became clear within months that no progress could be made because Anjou was as committed to his Catholicism as the Archduke Ferdinand had been in a similar situation more than a decade earlier. Once again the younger brother - in this case the Duke of Alençon - was proposed as an alternative suitor. However, on this occasion the suggestion hardly seemed worthy of serious consideration. At the time Alençon was a weakly youth of unprepossessing appearance. His face, including an unfashionable large and bulbous nose, was said to be seriously disfigured by the ravages of smallpox. Elizabeth felt no embarrassment at indicating that she could not contemplate a match with a boy who was twenty years her junior.

There the matter might have lain had not a fortuitous combination of circumstances dictated otherwise. From the French side there were two factors which made a renewal of the marriage proposal desirable. In 1574 Charles IX died and was succeeded by the Duke of Anjou who became Henry III. Alençon (who inherited his brother's title of Anjou and is thus referred to by some writers, although he will continue to be called Alençon here in order to avoid possible confusion) quickly established himself as a thorn in the new king's side by plotting with the enemies of the régime in the hope of winning himself additional powers. Both Henry III and his mother were therefore greatly attracted to the idea of marrying him off to Elizabeth as a way of getting him safely out of France. For his part, Alençon fancied becoming King-Consort of England as a way of laying his hands on the resources he needed to raise an army to fight alongside the Dutch rebels in the Netherlands, who had offered to make him their new ruler, against the King of Spain. Elizabeth and her closest advisers could also see potential political advantage in an

Alençon match. Besides the perennial hope that marriage would lead to the birth of an heir - still thought to be a possibility despite the fact that Elizabeth was advancing beyond the normal child-bearing years - both the queen and her leading councillors thought that a King-Consort fighting in the Netherlands could be manipulated to act in England's interests, whereas the Duke of Alençon acting independently might cause all manner of unwelcome international complications. Marriage would be the way of preventing Alençon becoming a 'loose cannon'.

For a time negotiations were conducted in the sort of desultory fashion that suggested neither side was intent on bringing them to a successful conclusion. Then, in January 1579 all was changed. Alençon sent Jean Simier, one of the most accomplished members of his household, to London to woo Elizabeth on his behalf. Simier was an immediate success. His grace and charm took the English court by storm, and his clever flattery entranced the queen, who started to act like a love-struck adolescent when in his company. The ground could not have been better prepared for Alençon to make a personal visit to England in August. Nor could the ten-day visit - the first by one of the queen's foreign suitors - have been a greater success. Elizabeth was smitten. The unflattering descriptions of Alençon's appearance were found to be exaggerated, his demeanour was judged to be that of a man who was passionately in love and who could not continue to live were he to be denied the object of his desire, and he made it engagingly clear that he was hers for the queen to command in every detail. By the time he returned to France the general opinion at court was that Elizabeth had definitely decided to marry him.

The news burst like a bombshell on the English political scene. Those who favoured the match were thrown onto the defensive by the virulence of the reaction of those who opposed it. The opponents were led and orchestrated by Leicester, who saw his position as one of the most influential men in the kingdom seriously threatened by the proposed marriage. Nearly all the cards lay in the opposition's hands. They were able to appeal to the Englishman's xenophobic hatred of the French, to capitalise on the Protestants' fears (rational and irrational) of Catholicism, and to pour ridicule on the idea of a 46-year-old woman planning to marry someone who was young enough to be her son. Both the pulpit and the printing press were used to whip up opposition to the match. The most famous of the publications which argued against the marriage was written by a respected lawyer, John Stubbs. In a period when most books and pamphlets did not have a title in the modern sense - the title page was normally used to give a description of what was to follow - Stubbs's pamphlet carried the name 'A gaping gulf wherein England is like to be swallowed by another French marriage if the Lord forbid not the bans by letting Her Majesty see the sin and punishment thereof'. It contained a large amount of reasoned argument, intermixed with invective and appeals to prejudice. Typical of the approach used was the description of Alençon as,

> this odd fellow, by birth a Frenchman, by profession a Papist, an
> atheist by conversion, an instrument in France of uncleanness, a fly
> worker in England for Rome and France in this present affair, a
> sorcerer by common voice and fame.

Alençon's supporters could not begin to counter the adverse publicity
among the population at large. There were no arguments they could
advance that stood any chance of competing with those of their
opponents. The best they could do was to work directly on the queen to
strengthen her resolve to proceed come what may. Fate had presented
them with one powerful weapon. The Earl of Leicester had recently
committed a huge error of judgement by secretly, and unbeknown to the
queen, marrying the dowager Countess of Essex. When Elizabeth was
told of this her anger was unrestrained. She felt that her friend had
committed the ultimate betrayal. Not only was Leicester banned from
court in the deepest of disgraces but, as those who had fed her with the
information had hoped, Elizabeth's determination to marry her 'frog'
(as she nicknamed Alençon with affectionate irony) was greatly
increased. The supporters of the marriage's other ploy was to fuel the
queen's resentment that numbers of her subjects had the effrontery to
speak out against a course of action that she regarded as being her
business alone. John Stubbs, in particular, was targeted. Not only was
she persuaded to take action against him on dubious legal grounds (it
was generally thought that the statute used had lapsed on Queen Mary's
death in 1558), but she was encouraged to allow the brutal sentence
passed on Stubbs and his printer to be carried out in a public ceremony.
Their right hands were cut off in front of a sullenly hostile crowd. This is
the clearest possible evidence that her judgement was seriously impaired
during this time.

   However, Elizabeth had not completely lost touch with political
reality. Her instincts told her that it would only be safe to proceed if her
Privy Council would advise her to go ahead. And this is what she
desperately wished them to do. She set things up so as to achieve the
desired result. Known opponents of the match were sent away and those
who remained were instructed to meet and to tender their advice one by
one (with names given) and in writing. The outcome was highly
disappointing to the queen. The majority sat on the fence, saying that
they would support the match if it was what Elizabeth wanted. In
essence the question was put back to the queen for her decision. This
was definitely not what she wanted. Twice more the Privy Council was
asked to deliberate and advise, but on both occasions the outcome was
the same - protestations of loyal support of whatever Elizabeth decided.
It was clear that the advice that was desired was not going to be
forthcoming. It was not going to be unreservedly recommended that the

marriage with Alençon go ahead. After these three inconclusive meetings of the Privy Council in October 1579 the queen seems to have accepted that the romance would not have a happy ending. Although all the right signals in favour of there being a wedding were given by her during a second visit from Alençon in 1581, Elizabeth was doing no more than playing a very enjoyable charade. Long before Alençon died in 1584 all pretence that the suit was still alive had been abandoned. With its demise any prospect that Elizabeth would eventually marry had disappeared.

8 Elizabeth's Attitude to Marriage

Dozens of historians have speculated in an attempt to identify what Elizabeth's views were about marriage. As a result a bewildering variety of explanations has been advanced, but none of them has carried total conviction. This is because certainty on this issue is unattainable. Not only is the surviving evidence contradictory - Elizabeth had much to say on the subject but often inspired guesswork is the only way of disentangling views that were expressed for effect from those that were genuinely held - but it also seems likely that her opinions were changeable and lacking in overall coherence. Therefore many writers have been seeking to discover logic and order where probably none ever existed. Despite this, the attempt to provide an explanation is worth making. Biographers quite naturally wish to disentangle their subject's views on what was one of the central issues of her life, and political historians consider that herein lies vital evidence about how Elizabeth approached her role as monarch.

There is strong evidence that Elizabeth accepted the prevailing belief that a woman's role, as ordained by God, was to marry and have children. However, it seems that she made a distinction between herself and ordinary women. Her view appears to have been that, because God had created her as a prince to rule over the people who were subject to the English and Irish crowns, she was in some way an honorary man - not in a sexual sense but as far as the ordering of society was concerned. This idea seems to have set up tensions within her that she was never able properly to resolve. As a result she was periodically dragged in opposite directions. At times she was content - and even exalted in the fact - not to have a marriage partner. Later in her life this was erected into the belief that this was so because she was in effect married to her people and therefore was not available to contract a normal human marriage. At other times she became convinced that it was her painful duty to take a husband and to become a mother as other women were. This was particularly the case when she found herself drawn to a man by a strong physical attraction, as with Dudley in 1559-60 and Alençon in 1579.

This mixture of confused and contradictory ideas might provide the key to much of Elizabeth's otherwise irrational and inexplicable behaviour over the issue of her marriage. This is especially so if one accepts the reasonable contention that from an early age she disliked, and was probably very fearful of, the very idea of being a wife and a mother (she would have seen the two as being inextricably linked). The concept of the 'joy of motherhood' does not belong to the sixteenth century when the act of bearing children was almost universally thought of as a painful and potentially life-threatening experience - one of the many ills that a woman might expect to have inflicted on her. It is likely that this perception was forced upon Elizabeth at a very impressionable age when, as a young teenager, she lost the only person who had been a real mother figure to her (Catherine Parr) in child-birth. In addition, the positive reasons for upper-class women to marry (to show obedience to their parents' wishes and to gain financial security) did not apply in Elizabeth's case. So she was just left with the negatives - the placing of oneself under the control of a husband, and the loss of most aspects of independence. It is therefore not to be wondered at that throughout her adult life she regularly exhibited an underlying distaste for marriage. Perhaps the most striking single piece of supporting evidence for this view is to be found in the oft-quoted words of the queen to her first parliament in 1559:

This shall be for me sufficient that a marble stone shall declare that a queen, having reigned such a time, lived and died a virgin.

What then does all this tell us about the way in which Elizabeth approached her task of being a monarch? One writer, in a most judicious use of the understatement, has suggested that her dynastic sense was not strong. The contrast with her father, who went to such great lengths to ensure the continuation of his line, is most striking. Elizabeth seems to have had no qualms about allowing herself to become the last of the Tudors. This fact, along with the way in which she acted over the succession, has been used by some historians to portray her as a self-centred egotist whose first (and often last) thought was to do what was in her own best interest and what fitted in with her personal desires, rather than thinking about what would benefit her country and its people.

However, it could be that this verdict is harsh and unfair. At first sight it does look as if Elizabeth consistently resisted the strongly voiced pleas of her people to take a husband and to produce an heir. Equally it appears that her vague promises to act when she thought the time was right were no more than stalling tactics designed to hide the truth that she had decided never to marry. However, the facts do not really bear out the case. Admittedly the idea of the queen marrying and having children was a straightforward one in theory, but it did not prove to be so in practice. Never was a suitable potential partner, who would have been acceptable to a majority of the English political classes, forthcoming. Certainly Elizabeth never refused to consider a prospective husband who was thought to be in the country's interests. And twice (in 1560 and 1579) she refrained from marriage for the sake of the country when her very strong personal inclination was to proceed. What is more, she was prepared to face the prospect of becoming a mother in her late forties (she was advised that it would be possible as she had not yet reached her menopause) despite the fact that the danger to herself would have been great. In the mid-1560s the Spanish ambassador reported her as saying,

> If I could appoint such a successor to the crown as would please me and the country, I would not marry, as it is a thing for which I have no inclination.

The implication of this is that Elizabeth was still prepared to marry for the sake of the country. There is good reason to think that she meant it, and that her failure ever to take a husband and produce an heir resulted from there never being a situation in which to do so would lead to more gains than losses for the country. It seems probable that the queen deserves much more credit for her handling of both the marriage and the succession issues than she has been given in recent times.

Making notes on 'Elizabeth I, Marriage and the Succession'

Your first task is to record the key facts on both the marriage and the succession issues. On the question of Elizabeth's marriage you need to make a note on each of the suitors. This should include i) the main events in the course of the suit, and ii) the reasons why it was not successful. Be sure to indicate dates so that you can build up a clear chronology of the events in your mind. The best way of recording the general facts about the succession would be to copy the genealogical table on page 104. You also need to make a note about the issues affecting Mary, Queen of Scots' claim to the throne.

A much more challenging task is the one that is really important - making notes about what can be learnt about Elizabeth from the way she acted over the two issues covered in the chapter. The notes would be most useful if you were able to describe the conclusions you have reached and why, rather than just summarising the points made in the text. But if this is more than you feel confident about doing at the moment, perhaps you could record your own conclusions during the revision phase of your course. You might find it a help in thinking through the issues if you were to divide these notes into two sections - what can be learnt about i) Elizabeth's personality and character, and ii) Elizabeth's performance as queen.

Answering essay questions on *'Elizabeth I, Marriage and the Succession'*

Examiners occasionally set questions that are restricted to the issues of the marriage and the succession, but you are much more likely to be given an opportunity to use what you have learnt from this chapter in answering a wider ranging question about Elizabeth and/or her performance as queen. That is why the second of the note-making tasks described above is of such vital importance.

Study the essay titles on the next page which are a mixture of both types of question.

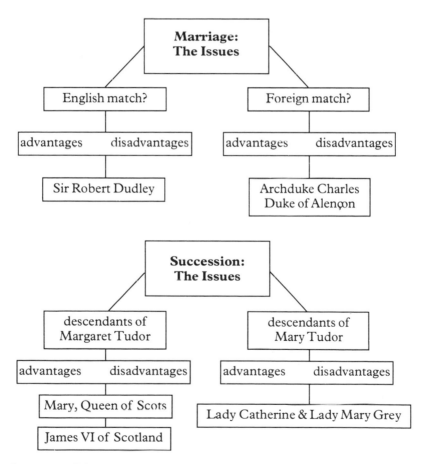

Summary - Elizabeth I, Marriage and the Succession

1   Why did Elizabeth I remain unmarried?
2   Why did the question of the succession stir up such strong feelings in England during the first half of Elizabeth I's reign?
3   Assess Elizabeth I's performance as Queen of England.
4   Did Elizabeth I's strengths outweigh her weaknesses?
5   Why have historians shown so much interest in whom Elizabeth I might have married and who might have succeeded her?
6   'Elizabeth I's success as a monarch has been greatly exaggerated.' Do you agree?

You are probably already aware that the three 'specific' questions are likely to appear on papers covering a limited time span, such as the years 1558-1603, whereas the three 'general' ones would probably feature in outline papers covering, for example, the whole of the Tudor and Stuart periods. One of the types of question clearly demands depth of knowledge and understanding on the student's part, while the other type requires breadth. Which is which?

The three 'specific' questions all begin with the word 'why'. As you know, the standard way of tackling such questions is to plan a sequence of paragraphs each dealing with a different cause. However, sometimes the wording of a question allows you to adopt an even better approach. Sometimes you can use the 'some say this, and some say that, but I think ...' plan, or a variant of it. In only one of questions 1, 2, and 5 would this approach work really well. Which one is it? One of the advantages of this type of plan is that it makes it easy to focus on the varying interpretations that have been advanced by different historians - an approach that almost always attracts high marks if it is done well. But beware! Most examiners are on the look out for name-droppers, and they tend to react negatively when they find one. So do not attempt to give the impression that you have more knowledge than you do by referring to a historian by name unless you have read something he/she has written or at least understand a fair amount about what he or she has done. Conversely, when you do name a historian, ensure that you include a well-chosen phrase or so to show that there is knowledge and understanding behind the reference you have made. That way you will not be thought to be a name-dropper.

The 'some say this ...' plan would work well with one of the 'general' questions. Which one?

Source-based questions on *'Elizabeth I, Marriage and the Succession'*

1 Elizabeth and the Parliament of 1563
Carefully read the extract from the speech made by Elizabeth to members of the parliament of 1563, given on page 105. Answer the following questions.

a)   The structure of this speech is complex and its meaning is vague and
     obscure. Why was this so? (6 marks)
b)   What is the implication of the statement, 'Of which two the last I
     think is best to be touched.'? (3 marks)
c)   What meaning was contained in the words 'for I had thought ... been
     denied you' (lines 5-7)? (2 marks)
d)   What would the audience probably have understood from the final
     sentence of the extract? (3 marks)
e)   What conclusions can be drawn from the fact that the speech was
     generally well received? (6 marks)

2 John Stubbs's Pamphlet, 1579

Carefully read the title and the extract from John Stubbs's pamphlet,
given on pages 112-13. Answer the following questions.
a)   What were 'the bans' referred to in the title of the pamphlet?
     (2 marks)
b)   Select two words or phrases from the title and explain why they
     would have been likely to offend Elizabeth. (4 marks)
c)   What was being implied or referred to in the phrase 'an instrument
     in France of uncleanness'? (2 marks)
d)   What reason might Stubbs have had for describing Alençon as a
     sorcerer? (3 marks)
e)   What can be deduced about Elizabeth's state of mind at the time
     from the way she handled the matter of the Stubbs pamphlet?
     (4 marks)

3 Elizabeth's Attitude towards her own Marriage

Carefully read the statement made by Elizabeth to parliament in 1559
(page 115) and her comment made to the Spanish ambassador (page
116). Answer the following questions.
a)   Paraphrase the statement made to parliament, so as to make clear its
     meaning. (4 marks)
b)   What does the comment made to the Spanish ambassador imply
     about Elizabeth's intentions and the reasons for them? (5 marks)
c)   What does the comment made to the Spanish ambassador imply
     about Elizabeth's views about how her successor would be chosen?
     (2 marks)
d)   Why do historians normally treat Elizabeth's statements made to
     ambassadors with particular caution? (4 marks)

CHAPTER 7

The Later Years

1 Introduction

From about 1930 to about 1980 the orthodox interpretation of the history of Elizabethan England, based on the work of J.E. Neale and Conyers Read, remained largely unchallenged. During this period it was almost universally accepted that the final decade or so of the queen's long reign (often loosely referred to as 'the 1590s') was a period of increasing political instability which marked a sad decline from the admirable state of affairs that had prevailed until then. The contrast being made was between a 'good' arrangement which existed especially during the middle portion of the reign and a 'bad' situation which developed during the later years and which tarnished Elizabeth's otherwise fine reputation. Since about 1980 various aspects of the orthodox interpretation have been vigorously challenged by a wide variety of historians. Between them they have cast considerable doubt on the old orthodoxy. As most of the recent studies have pointed in the same general direction, it has become usual to refer to their collective findings as the 'revisionist interpretation'. This has become common practice despite the fact that the use of this phrase might encourage the belief that the views of the revisionists have a collective coherence that they actually lack. It is true that many of the research historians who are designated as belonging to this revisionist school share a number of general interpretations of the period, but most of them have been working completely independently on matters of detail and would not necessarily subscribe to the views advanced by those researching different aspects of the politics of the final years. Therefore it might be safest to think of the revisionist interpretation of the period 1590-1603 as a collection of related but unco-ordinated contributions to a lively debate that is still on-going rather than as a unitary and completed challenger to the 'old' orthodoxy.

So the task for the student is more complicated than deciding between two fully fledged competing interpretations. What is needed is an assessment of the extent to which the findings of members of the revisionist school have discredited the old orthodoxy and have replaced it with a more convincing way of looking at the period. In order to make this judgement it is necessary both to understand the old orthodoxy and to appreciate the ways in which it has been called into question. This chapter has been designed with these requirements in mind.

2 The Old Orthodoxy: the 1570s and 1580s

At the heart of the old orthodoxy was the contrast made between the political situation of the 1570s and 1580s and that of the 1590s. The former period was portrayed as the era of Elizabethan stability during which the régime was secure because it was popular and because political forces were in a state of balance. It was claimed that the popularity was widespread among all sections of society.

Partly this public approval was a matter of the queen being widely thought of as a great leader who was worthy of her people's support and affection. The evidence of her subjects' devotion to Elizabeth was plentiful. Direct evidence was supplied, for example, by the many surviving accounts written by those who had witnessed the queen's graciousness towards her people. Her public appearances were consciously arranged so as to show her in all her majesty - especially fine attire was the order of the day for all involved, and elaborate ceremonial was adopted wherever it would create the maximum impression. Her ability to judge just the right moments to abandon protocol in order to show warmth to the ordinary people was a particularly striking feature of her forays outside of her court.

Indirect evidence of the esteem in which Elizabeth was held is even easier to come by. This is because she was the subject of one of the earliest attempts to create a cult of personality. From the time of her entry into London following the death of Queen Mary in 1558 it became routine for her to be celebrated in poems, plays and pictures as the savour of her nation. Official blessing was often given to these efforts by the royal printer being instructed to publish the best literary pieces, and by those who were thought to have done particularly well being presented to the queen. In exceptional cases those who glorified Elizabeth were even rewarded by being granted an annual pension for life. The most renowned of these pensioners was Edmund Spenser, the author of *The Faerie Queen*. This massive, unfinished epic poem - Spenser died in 1598 having completed and published (in 1590 and 1594) only 6 of the intended 12 'books' - is generally regarded as being the outstanding English poetic work of the sixteenth century. This is despite the fact that its archaic style (it was even thought to be written in old-fashioned language at the time) and over elaboration of content make it inaccessible to all but the most determined present-day reader. *The Faerie Queen* was an account of the chivalric exploits of the knights of the imaginary court of Gloriana, the Queen of Faeryland, and was told in allegorical form. It was very clear to the people of the time that the queen, in whom all virtue was said to reside, was intended to be Elizabeth because allegorical pieces in which she was given the name of Gloriana were commonplace by the 1590s. Equally commonplace, at least in the houses of the gentry, were portraits of the queen. The fact that most of these were nearly identical, presenting the queen as youthful and majestic, was not a coincidence. Part of the official encouragement of the cult of personality was the provision of an approved portrait of Elizabeth so that those who wished to publicise their patriotism by hanging a picture of their monarch in their homes could arrange to have it copied by an artist of their choice. A similar approach was revealed by the encouragement of public celebrations on 17 November, the anniversary of the queen's accession to the throne. This began in the early 1570s. From 1576 the date was made a public holiday on which church bells were rung. Most communities arranged a public celebration to mark the day.

In the old orthodoxy there was no suggestion that the political balance of the 1570s and 1580s was in any sense a natural occurrence. Elizabeth was given most of the credit for bringing it about. It was said that her major success was in ensuring that no section of the political classes was sufficiently alienated from the régime to tempt it to join in any of the plots against her that, given the nature of the political system of the time in which there was no lawful way for opposition to her to express itself with any hope of success, were bound to surface occasionally. This was primarily done by steering a middle course in religious matters, and in particular by refusing to persecute the members of the many influential Catholic families who remained true to their faith for decades after the establishment of a Protestant national Church in 1559. Not only was a blind eye turned to the widespread disregard of the law whereby those who did not attend the Church of England were to be fined, but those who advocated moving the Anglican Church further away from its Catholic roots were also given the message that their efforts would not be successful. Elizabeth had made the conscious decision that those of her subjects who remained committed to the 'old' faith would not be driven into opposition to the régime on grounds of conscience.

The old orthodoxy also argued that a vital part of the political balance of the 1570s and 1580s was the way in which the strength of the factions was kept in near equilibrium. Once again Elizabeth was given the credit for establishing and maintaining this situation. It was claimed that she encouraged factions so that she would always have a choice of ministers and policies to support, and that she managed the factions well by rewarding each of them sufficiently to make their leaders feel that they had the prospect of even greater successes in the future as long as they continued to play the game by the queen's unwritten rules. The most important of these rules was that in the last resort - when the full repertory of deception and evasion had been exhausted - the queen's authority would be respected and her instructions would be obeyed. This skill in managing factions, it was said, had been learned from experience during the 1560s when the situation had been allowed to get out of hand for a time, and had been put to the test in 1569 when Elizabeth's courage and persistence had been all that had prevented political disaster from befalling the régime. The orthodox view was that thereafter Cecil's faction and Leicester's faction, in particular, had shared the spoils of the patronage system and had influenced policy sufficiently equally for contentment with the *status quo* to be the prevailing sentiment.

3 The Old Orthodoxy: the 1590s

The old orthodoxy presented a stark contrast between the balance and stability of the middle portion of Elizabeth's reign and the imbalance and potential instability of the later years. The dividing line was said to be about 1590. This date was chosen because it was the time when many of the leading political figures of the former period died - most notably Leicester in 1588, Walsingham in 1590, and Sir Christopher Hatton in 1591 - and when the two major political figures of the final phase of the reign, the Earl of Essex and Sir Robert Cecil, emerged into the limelight. It was argued that it was the loss of the moderating influence of Leicester in particular and its replacement by Essex's dangerous recklessness that caused the dramatic shift in political climate, and that this was added to by the fading glory of a noticeably aging and less competent monarch whose popularity was declining for a variety of reasons. This decline in popularity was thought to have occurred both in Court circles and in the country at large. The cause for the disenchantment at the country's political centre was claimed to be the failure of the financial benefits of patronage to keep pace with either inflation or the increase in the number of those seeking to boost their incomes from the fount of royal munificence. The nation's social elite was also thought to have been placed under additional financial pressure by parliamentary taxation, becoming for the first time virtually a permanent feature of life, as opposed to being an exceptional circumstance as it had traditionally been in the past. Among the population at large the causes of discontent were portrayed as a mixture of the avoidable and the unavoidable. The avoidable were those that arose from actions taken by the government, foremost among which were the increased prices of many everyday goods resulting from the granting of monopolies (see page 28) and the fear of being forced to serve as a soldier or a sailor in one of the many foreign expeditions that were mounted during the 1590s. It was widely and correctly believed that selection for military service abroad was almost the same as being issued with a death warrant. Added to these government-inspired ills were the hardships caused by three consecutive poor harvests between 1594 and 1596 - one harvest failure followed by a good or even a reasonable year was commonplace and could generally be managed, but a sequence of seriously below average yields resulted in widespread hunger among the poorer half of the population, and even to isolated pockets of starvation. It was only human nature for 'them' (those in authority) to be blamed for not being able to remedy the situation.

It has sometimes been suggested that by the late-1590s so many people were disillusioned with the régime that it was in a very weak state, and was vulnerable to even a half-hearted attack. This was because it was estimated that relatively few people would have come to its defence, in clear contrast to the situation a decade earlier when a majority of the landowning class was thought to have been prepared to take action against any *coup* designed to further the interests of Mary, Queen of Scots. It has also been claimed that the régime did in fact nearly succumb to those who had lost sympathy with it. This contention has arisen from studies of the career of a remarkable man, Robert Devereux, second Earl of Essex.

3 Earl of Essex

a) Background

Robert Devereux became the Earl of Essex at the age of nine in 1576 when his father died during an unsuccessful attempt to revive his financial fortunes by founding large-scale English settlements on confiscated land in Ireland. The Devereux were proud of their ancestry, even if it depended heavily on advantageous marriages which had brought traces of royal blood into the family. They thought of themselves as belonging to the very select group of descendants from the medieval English aristocracy.

Two years after his father's death Essex's mother married the Earl of Leicester. This meant that the young aristocrat grew up at the very heart of English political life. By the time he became a full-time courtier at the age of 20 in 1587 he had already made a name for himself. While serving in a senior position under his step-father in the English army in the Netherlands he had been knighted for distinguished acts of bravery. Within a few months he not only established himself within the small circle of Elizabeth's favourites and secured appointment as the queen's Master of Horse when Leicester relinquished the post, but he was also awarded the most prestigious honour the queen had to bestow. He was made a member of the Order of the Garter. The mastership of the horse assured him of an income of £1,500 a year and guaranteed him a daily audience with the queen. It is therefore not surprising that when Leicester died in 1588 Essex was widely thought of as his natural successor.

b) The Man

In memorable words J.E. Neale described Essex as 'the incarnation of poetry, a young aristocrat of irresistible attraction, impulsive and generous, the chivalrous courtly knight of romance'. And indeed he was truly charismatic. His appeal was almost universal. Women virtually fell at his feet and most of the men with whom he had dealings fell under the spell of the gracious condescension which flowed naturally from his lightly assumed air of superiority. To the population at large - at first in the capital but then further afield - he appeared to be every inch a natural leader. He was the type of public figure around whom people could weave the fantasies of their choice. For many he was the person they would willingly die for. Had there been a tabloid press at the time he would have featured in it on almost a daily basis. He drew people to him in a way that was unique for a commoner in sixteenth-century England.

However, if one were tempted to liken Essex to a Greek god, it would have to be said that he was one with feet of clay. The second sentence of Neale's description is a masterful piece of low-key demolition. He wrote that, 'All the qualities for a brilliant career were his, save judgement, an

Earl of Essex, after Marcus Gheeraerts the Younger, c 1596

equable temper and discretion'. He might have added that Essex had a seemingly irresistible urge to self-destruct. Those who believe in, or like to appear to believe in, telling fortunes from the stars would probably claim that he was born to be a tragic figure and that there was an inevitability about the course of his career. In addition, students of the occult might derive satisfaction from identifying a certain symmetry in the fact that for every one of Essex's positive qualities there appears to have been an equal and opposite negative one. The generosity with which he habitually treated those who sought his assistance was matched by an irresponsible disregard for the interests of those to whom he owed money. He accumulated debts at a breakneck speed - on average each year he spent the equivalent of an average peer's income, more than he received - and he had no idea how he would ever recompense those who supplied him with goods and services on credit. The other side of his easy and gracious authority over those who recognised his superiority were his petulant, vindictive and ill-judged attempts to do down those who did not act with subservience towards him. Even his friends were sometimes amazed at the extent of his over-reaction when the treatment he considered his due was not forthcoming. A typical, although extreme, example of what was really his paranoia was his attempt to have Sir Walter Ralegh executed for daring to lead an assault on an enemy position when he, as the commander, was absent from the scene, thereby robbing him of the glory of the victory. In the event, Ralegh was spared but all mention of the successful action was omitted from the official account of the expedition. In his dealings with the queen, Essex, the dutiful subject and dedicated slave of courtly love, on occasions became the spoilt child who attempted to have his own way even when he was told in the plainest of terms that enough was enough. And time after time his selfless conduct in the field of battle, when he persevered against all the odds, was mirrored by similar persistence on the domestic political scene. However, an approach that is described as courageous in warfare is sometimes highly inappropriate when transferred to meetings of the Privy Council or to attempts to win favours from the queen. If Essex was valiant in battle he was often an inept bully when operating in the realm of politics.

c) His Career

Throughout his twenties, in the decade following 1587, Essex established and maintained a well-deserved reputation as an *enfant terrible*. He consistently acted outrageously, overplaying his hand with reckless frequency but always managing (by luck rather than judgement) to avoid the ultimate disaster of death or disgrace. He relied on the fact that the queen's enormous affection for him - in many ways she thought of him as the son she had never had - would be strong enough to save him from the consequences of his actions, and he was proved right over and over again. In 1589 he left the Court and against Elizabeth's explicit instructions joined the naval expedition designed to prevent the Spanish mounting a second armada against England. An amount of pre-planning and the speed with which he journeyed to the West Country and set sail ahead of the main fleet allowed him to evade the order to return that the queen sent after him long enough for him to enhance his reputation as a valiant man of action. On his return Elizabeth accepted his penitence with a scarcely concealed amusement that seemed to say 'but boys will be boys'. In 1591, when an expedition to France was being arranged to support Henry IV in his efforts to gain control of the country by overcoming his Catholic opponents and their Spanish allies, Essex managed to prevail on the queen to give him sole command of the enterprise. Although he blatantly disregarded the orders he had been given for the use to which his army was to be put, having returned to Court on a flying visit, he was able to persuade Elizabeth to give him a second chance and to extend the army's period of service abroad. Despite the facts that the further period of activity was equally fruitless, that none of the intended objectives of the expedition were achieved, and that the only benefit seemed to be to Essex's reputation as a man of importance, no action was taken against the commander who had so thoughtlessly squandered his monarch's scant resources. In 1595, 1596 and 1597 combined military and naval expeditions were mounted against Spain with Essex in joint command but, apart from the temporary seizure of Cadiz on the first occasion, it would not be unfair to describe the ventures as expensive failures. However, such was the patriotic mood of the country that careful publicity was able to portray Essex in a heroic light. He was generally thought to be a military leader of distinction, and by far the finest commander that England possessed. In this he seems to have deluded himself as well as many other people.

There is little doubt that in the early-1590s Elizabeth hoped to do in internal politics what she had done 30 years previously when she had managed Leicester's translation into a leading politician with a powerful following. She groomed Essex, as a generation earlier she had prepared his step-father, for governmental responsibility. In 1593 she thought that he was ready to fill a leading political role and she made him a member of her Privy Council. During the period of Essex's preparation she attempted to restrict the power of the Cecil faction so that her young favourite would stand a chance of establishing himself in a position of effective parity. When Sir Francis Walsingham had died in 1590 Burghley had wished the vacant Principal Secretary post to go to one of his supporters, preferably to his son Sir Robert Cecil. Elizabeth had denied him this and in typical fashion had refused to make a decision. As a consequence the position remained unfilled. The best arrangement that Burghley was able to negotiate was that he would do most of the Secretary's work himself (although he was in his seventies and in poor health) but that he would be helped by his son in a semi-official capacity.

For a few months after his appointment to the Privy Council Essex made himself act in a more responsible manner and it seemed as if the queen's strategy might prove successful. But the leopard soon proved that it was unable to change its spots. Parity with the Cecil faction was not something that Essex was prepared to accept. He wished both to dominate it and to be seen to be doing so. One way in which he did this was by making very public pronouncements about whom he wished to see appointed to a number of vacant positions that were in the queen's gift, and on each occasion his preferred candidate was not the one that the Cecils were known to favour. He refused all offers of a compromise and, although Elizabeth delayed making decisions in an effort to avoid having to choose between her old counsellor and her young favourite, he insisted on staking his reputation on the appointment of people whom the queen had made clear she either disliked or thought were unsuitable. Essex made it known to those close to him - and the whole of the Court had a fair idea what was going on - that he intended to force Elizabeth to do as he wished. In the circumstances the queen was remarkably patient and did her best not to make Essex's position untenable. But she was determined not to be bullied by him on a regular basis. She gave way on a number of points that affected her favourite personally, including making him Earl Marshall (the titular commander of her armies) in 1597 so that he would retain his formal precedence over the Lord Admiral who had recently been promoted to an earldom, but she made none of the appointments he had so publicly advocated. In fact, normally after a lengthy delay during which Essex could have modified his position, she almost invariably chose the candidate whom Burghley favoured. It seems that this was done partly in an attempt to bring Essex into line, although it was generally the case that the person appointed was the one whom the queen favoured - which is why Burghley had supported him in the first place. The exception to this rule was the much delayed appointment of Sir Robert Cecil as Principal Secretary in 1597. Historians have often cited the way in which this was done as a typical example of Elizabeth's sensitivity towards Essex's feelings - Cecil received the prize for which he had long worked while Essex was abroad on the so-called Islands Expedition, just as he had been made a Privy Councillor while Essex was in France in 1591. However, it could equally well be argued that this way of acting provides evidence that the queen was more than a little afraid of her favourite as, of course, he intended her to be.

Whatever Elizabeth's motives were for behaving as she did, the result could not have been to her liking, for instead of Essex learning his lesson he became more and more desperate to prove to the world that he was politically powerful. Thanks especially to historians who have researched what was happening in the localities during the 1590s, it has become clear that to a much greater extent than ever before members of the gentry were being pressurised into declaring themselves for one or other of the main factions. The pace in this was undoubtedly being set by Essex (it seems that the Cecils merely acted defensively) whose 'organisers' routinely employed bully-boy tactics. Scarcely veiled threats were used against those over whom Essex had economic influence, while some people who were independent enough to consider themselves to be neutral were told that they must either declare themselves for Essex or they would be considered to be against him. There is disagreement about how widespread this 'politicisation' of the localities was, but it is clear that in some districts Essex's supporters adopted what appears to have been a warlike stance towards their opponents.

There is no direct evidence about the stages by which Elizabeth's attitude towards Essex changed but it seems that the key decision was made in July 1598. Up until then the queen had been prepared to give him chance after chance and to overlook indiscretion after indiscretion in the hope that he would eventually settle down, just as his step-father had done. But the events surrounding the choice of commander to lead the expedition to restore English control of Ireland following the revolt of the Earl of Tyrone resulted in Elizabeth deciding, undoubtedly reluctantly, that her erring favourite would be allowed just one more opportunity to restore her faith in him. Given the circumstances in which the decision was made, it is highly surprising that he was allowed even that. The situation arose from a discussion between the queen and a small group of her military advisers, including Essex, about how matters in Ireland were to be handled. Elizabeth favoured the use of an army of modest size under the command of a 'second-line' general, while Essex argued strongly for the sending of the largest possible force under his command. When it appeared that the queen was not going to be persuaded by his reasoning, Essex subjected her to verbal abuse in a most offensive manner. At this Elizabeth flew into a rage and physically attacked her abuser - contemporary accounts describe her as 'boxing his ears'. Essex in his turn lost his temper and moved to draw his sword. Although he was restrained from committing what must have been regarded as an act of treason had it happened, he stormed from Court announcing that he was not prepared to be insulted in this way by anyone, even a queen.

Once the dust had settled it seemed that he had once again been triumphant. Not only was he given charge of the expedition to Ireland, but he was also allowed to make it the largest force (16,000 infantry and 1,300 cavalry) to be sent abroad during Elizabeth's reign. But the extent of his success made it all the more dangerous for him. It is likely that it confirmed Elizabeth in her determination that Essex must prove himself to be a loyal and obedient subject in Ireland, or else! He was despatched in March 1599 with very clear instructions about what he should and should not do. But almost from the outset he disregarded the orders he had been given. Most significantly of all he failed to head north from

Dublin to confront the Earl of Tyrone in Ulster. Instead he wasted the campaigning season in a series of pointless forays into central and southern Ireland, only heading northwards when his army was too weak and when the year was too advanced for him to be able to achieve anything of note. He then compounded his sin of omission with two more sins of commission. Instead of fighting Tyrone he made a truce with him, and contrary to an explicit instruction he left Ireland without permission in September and returned to London to justify his actions to the queen. This time Elizabeth was not prepared to be forgiving. Presumably Essex had expected a frosty reception at first, but as weeks turned into months and months into more than a year and the queen was still not prepared to smile upon him, he reached the conclusion that she would have to be forced to restore him to favour.

Essex seems not to have thought out clearly how this was to be done, nor to have calculated what the implications of attempting to coerce the queen with physical force might be. Because he was denied access to the Court he decided that he must take it over by force and compel Elizabeth to make him her sole adviser. But, once it became clear that any element of surprise had been lost, he formed only the vaguest of replacement plans for carrying out his armed coup. He thought that if he and a handful of his closest friends rode through the streets of London announcing that his life was in danger and calling on the people to protect him, he would soon gather together a sufficiently large following to be able to make an irresistible assault on the Court. When, on 8 February 1601, he attempted to put his plan into operation he found that his calls for assistance went unanswered. The London authorities blocked his route to the Court and he was forced to return to his house where he was subsequently arrested. By the end of the month he had, to his evident surprise, been charged with treason, tried, and executed. At the age of 34 he had paid the ultimate price for misjudging what he could and could not get away with.

d) An 'Old Orthodox' Assessment

For historians who accepted the old orthodoxy about the 1590s, Essex was a clear-cut example of someone snatching defeat from the jaws of victory. Their implication has been that overall it was almost more difficult for him to fail than it would have been for him to succeed. According to this interpretation his strategy of dominating the queen through confrontation was workable and only ended in tragedy because he was incompetent in pressing home his advantage between 1599 and 1601. The evidence that can be assembled to support this contention is impressive. There are the numerous occasions between 1589 and 1598 on which he successfully imposed his will on Elizabeth, often by acting in a way that contradicted instructions he had been given and subsequently being excused for his disobedience, or even more dramatically by forcing through decisions, such as over the arrangements for the Irish expedition, that were known to be contrary to the preferred royal policy. Central to this line of argument is the perception of Elizabeth in the 1590s as being a virtually spent force who was only capable of occasional struggles to free herself from bondage to the man in whom she had invested what remained of her emotional energy. Equally important to this interpretation is the judgement that Essex could, and probably should, have mounted a successful *coup* once he became aware that his conduct of affairs in Ireland was likely to lead to his disgrace. It has been suggested that while he was still in Ireland he could have decided to transport a few thousand of his men to the coast of Wales and then to have marched on London, gathering a sizable number of young gentry to his colours along the way (many of his most committed supporters lived in Wales or the neighbouring counties of England), and that had he done so he would have found nobody willing to resist him. It has also been maintained that, having failed to seize this opportunity, he could still have gathered around him in London a sufficient number of youthful supporters from other parts of the country to make it unnecessary to rely on the apprentices of the capital - the cause of his eventual undoing. The fact that he did neither of these things has been put down to a mixture of incompetence and over-confidence.

4 Revisionist Views: the 1570s and 1580s

The revisionist contribution to our understanding of the politics of the middle years of Elizabeth's reign has been relatively modest. There has been no presentation of a radical new interpretation. Rather there has been a request for a shift of emphasis. It has been suggested that the much-vaunted 'Elizabethan stability' has been exaggerated and misrepresented - the exaggeration being both over the extent to which the members of the landowning elite were united in support of the régime, and over the degree to which the leading politicians co-operated with one another, and the misrepresentation being over the queen's part in establishing and maintaining a balance between the factions. Although the case has not yet been proved, and probably never will be because of the absence of relevant evidence, it seems reasonable to speculate on the basis of the panic into which leading ministers sometimes descended that a significant minority of the gentry were sympathetic to those, especially Mary, Queen of Scots, who wished to alter the balance (if not the nature) of the régime. And there is no doubt that the commitment of the 'pro-Protestant' ministers (especially Leicester and Walsingham) to any idea of consensus politics became very strained from time to time when the queen clamped down on Protestant activists at home or refused to provide financial or military support to Protestant rebels abroad. There have also been challenges to the claim that Elizabeth should be credited with having formed and implemented a conscious plan to 'balance' the political forces around her. Although these have not been totally convincing, they have at least raised the possibility that the historians of the old orthodoxy sometimes thought they had found evidence of a pre-planned strategy when what they were actually looking at was a gut-reaction decision.

However, it should not be imagined that the work of revisionists on this period is inconsequential. It may not have necessitated a fundamental re-evaluation of the orthodox view but it has called into question one half of the traditional sharp contrast between the politics of the 1570s and 1580s and those of the 1590s, and that of course is its significance for this chapter. If it can be shown that the preceding period was not as 'balanced' as was once thought and that the queen was not quite the puppet-master of popular repute when in her prime, it may be that the final years of the Elizabethan period were not the sad decline that traditional interpretations have represented them as being. Perhaps the change was less dramatic than the old orthodox view would have us believe it was.

5 Revisionist Views: the 1590s

Although there clearly remains much research still to be done, it has already been established by revisionist historians that the Elizabethan régime was not on the verge of collapse at any time during its final years. It is possible to assert this because persuasive arguments have already been produced to discredit each of the major predictions of doom that were advanced by historians who supported the old orthodoxy. Some of the factors said to have dangerously weakened the régime have been dismissed with surprising ease. For example, it has been shown that the harsh economic conditions of the mid-1590s led to very little public disorder and that where there was a suggestion that the 'commons' should rise up to overthrow the government because it was not doing enough to ameliorate the situation the amount of support that was forthcoming was derisory. Similarly, the widespread public discontent that built up against monopolies between 1597 and 1601 seems to have dissipated rapidly once the queen revoked the most oppressive of them. In fact, it appears that each of the causes of general discontent with the régime - economic hardship, heavy taxation and war weariness in particular - produced a considerable amount of grumbling but did not stir more than the odd individual to take action in an attempt to replace the government.

A similar picture emerges when the key issues relating to politics are investigated. The three central contentions of the old orthodoxy in this area - that an ageing queen lost her grip on events, that the bitter rivalry between the Cecil and Essex factions destabilised the régime at its heart and in the localities, and that Essex could have led a successful *coup* in

1601 had he made fewer mistakes - have all been shown to be at best contentious. They have not yet been convincingly discredited but they have all been revealed as open to serious doubt. Although it is possible that future research will reinstate them to their former primacy, the prospect of this happening is remote.

A number of arguments have been advanced suggesting that Elizabeth did not experience a significant decline in her political skills during the later years of her reign. As might be expected, these have concentrated on reinterpreting the way in which she managed Essex and the problems that he posed. In its most complimentary form this line of argument has maintained that the queen handled this difficult situation positively well, displaying a mature wisdom in keeping the door open for her favourite to settle down into a responsible minister for as long as possible - it would have been a great waste had the most personable leader of his generation been lost to royal service - while at the same time ensuring that the smooth working of the government machine was not upset by his petulant behaviour. In particular, attention has been drawn to the strength of character she displayed on numerous occasions by standing up to his persistent demands that his wishes, for example over appointments, be met. An important element of this interpretation is the claim that she handled affairs especially skilfully between September 1599 and February 1601, when she was careful not to allow Essex grounds for appealing to public sympathy as somebody who was being harshly treated, and when she slowly tightened a noose around him - for example by refusing to renew his farm of sweet wines which was his single largest source of income - so that he was faced with the prospect of either remaining inactive and seeing his influence ebb away or committing himself to rash action from a position of weakness and probably destroying himself.

Plausible as the revisionist interpretations of Elizabeth's actions during the 1590s are, they are in no sense water-tight. They can be regarded as possible or even probable, depending on one's 'feel' for the issue, but they cannot be taken as certain. After all, it would not be difficult to construct less flattering interpretations of the queen's actions that still fitted all the known facts. But at least it does seem impossible to maintain that she was merely a shadow of her former self. Even if those who would wish us to believe that she was still near the top of her form have been guilty of reading consistency and prior planning into a situation where there was only reacting to circumstances, they have at least cast real doubt on the view that Elizabeth was in significant decline during the final 15 years of her life.

Equally the old orthodox view that the political scene in the 1590s was characterised by destabilising in-fighting which resulted in the Cecil faction securing a near monopoly of power and left the Essex faction with little option but to attempt to save its position by violent action, seems less convincing than it once did. In particular, greater emphasis has been placed on the abundant evidence of Essex and the Cecils working in co-operation, and on the way in which the Cecils made a conscious effort not to shut out their rivals. For example, they were often prepared to meet Essex more than half-way over issues, especially over matters of patronage where the appointment of a 'neutral' candidate was frequently recommended. In addition, further work on what was happening in the localities has raised the possibility that the division of the gentry into pro-Cecil and pro-Essex groups that was occurring in much of Wales, for example, was the exception rather than the rule. Even if at some time in the future this view were to be found to down-grade the 'divisive' interpretation too far, it is very unlikely that it will ever be accepted that the spread of Court divisions into the counties was a general phenomenon of the 1590s. Therefore the contention that by 1600 England was a country ready to slide into civil war seems to be discredited beyond recall. No attempt has been made to deny that at times factional rivalry was more intense than it had been since the mid-1560s, but it has been suggested that the contention that this dangerously undermined the régime is an exaggeration.

Revisionists have also doubted whether Essex was ever in a position to carry out a successful coup. By its very nature, of course, the case is not one that can either be proved or disproved. Because it is about a hypothetical situation the best that can be hoped for is informed speculation. Nevertheless, the issue is of historical significance as the conclusions reached about it will influence judgements about the wider question of the stability or otherwise of the late-Elizabethan régime. Those who favour a revisionist interpretation on this point freely admit that Essex exercised an amazing drawing power, especially among the younger generation, and that he had built up a clientage that was numerically the strongest of the Elizabethan age. However, they reject the view that this position could ever have been turned into support for an armed seizure of power. The evidence that can be assembled to substantiate this point of view mainly has to do with the way in which Essex was perceived by many people, including numbers of his supporters. It appears that much as people admired and were in awe of him, there was a widespread feeling that he was reckless and wrong-headed. For example, numerous attempts were made (in vain) by his friends to persuade him that his strategy of trying to brow-beat the queen was likely to end in disaster and that he would be better advised to submit to her will and to use the love she had for him as a lever to extract the bounty he sought. This ambivalent attitude is well illustrated in a statement made by Sir Robert Cecil during Essex's trial in February 1601.

1 My Lord of Essex, the difference between you and me is great. For wit, I give you preeminence: you have it abundantly. For nobility I also give you place: I am not noble, yet a gentleman. I am no

swordsman: there also you have the odds. But I have innocence,
5 conscience, truth and honesty to defend me against the slander and
sting of slanderous tongues, and in this court I stand as an upright
man, and your lordship as a delinquent.

It seems that many of those who were prepared to follow him in normal circumstances were not carried along by him in his more extreme behaviour. This situation is claimed to be exemplified by what happened in Ireland in September 1599 when, circumstantial evidence would suggest, Essex wished to return to England accompanied by a strong armed force, but was persuaded against the idea by those who were unprepared to put their heads in the noose by joining him. And, of course, the miserable support that was forthcoming during the coup fiasco itself would seem to prove the point. It certainly appears reasonable to speculate that the more 'solid' members of Essex's following were unprepared to go along with him once he stepped outside the law.

The sum total of revisionist views about the politics of the 1590s is that they were characterised much more by continuity than by change. Of course, it is not suggested that there was no significant change - the death of formerly major figures and the emergence of others to replace them ensured that all would not remain the same - but it is contended that the element of continuity in the form of a monarch whose political skills remained at a high level and who continued to enjoy the general support of the political classes was by far the more significant. However, as with so much about the government and politics of Elizabethan England, the debate continues. And while this state of uncertainty remains there is plenty of opportunity for the well informed student to formulate points of view of his or her own.

Making notes on 'The Later Years'

Two sections of your notes on this chapter - 'the old orthodox interpretation' and 'revisionist views' - can be of the straightforward 'summary of what has been read' type. As always with this sort of note making, the best way of avoiding recording excessive detail and of keeping the task within reasonable bounds is to make rules about the most you will allow yourself to write. The more experienced a note-maker you are the stricter the rules can afford to be. For instance, a realistic target for somebody nearing the end of an advanced course might be one generalisation (in the form of a simple sentence) and one example per paragraph. Like all sensible rules they will need to be broken from time to time, but only with good reason!

When you are making the third section of your notes (under a heading such as 'What I think') you should spend much more time deciding what to write than you do in writing it. This is because your task here is to make up your own mind about how far the old orthodox interpretation has been replaced by the views of the revisionists. At each stage of the argument you need to record what you think and why you think it. You can afford to be relaxed with yourself about how much you write in this section. In fact, it would be no bad thing if these notes ended up looking rather like an essay.

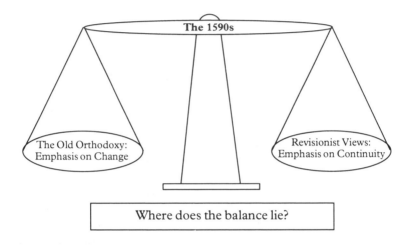

The 1590s

The Old Orthodoxy: Emphasis on Change

Revisionist Views: Emphasis on Continuity

Where does the balance lie?

Summary - The Later Years

Answering essay questions on 'The Later Years'

It is possible - especially if you have studied Elizabeth I's reign in depth rather than as part of an outline course - that you will be faced with a question about the Earl of Essex. If you wish to prepare yourself to answer such a question, re-read the advice on writing about Burghley and Leicester on page 73 and apply the same ideas to Essex. However, the probability is that any essay question you will encounter on *'The Final Years'* will focus on the controversy about how far this period was a time of political crisis for England. And, as with the questions on *'Elizabeth and Parliament'* discussed on page 94, the central issue to be discussed is likely to be the relative strengths of the 'old orthodox' and the 'revisionist' interpretations.

To develop your skills in analysing questions of this type further - or possibly to check that your skills are as sound as you think they are - consider each of the following questions and identify precisely what the examiner is requiring you to do. In question 4, what assumption will need to be explored in detail?

1 Was the Elizabethan régime in danger of collapse at any time between 1590 and 1603?
2 How far did Elizabeth I lose control of the political scene during the last 15 years of her life?
3 'A tired régime.' How accurate a description is this of English government in the 1590s?
4 To what extent was Elizabeth I responsible for the political instability of her later years?

Source-based questions on 'The Later Years'

1 The Earl of Essex
Study the portrait of the Earl of Essex on page 125 and carefully read Sir Robert Cecil's comments about him given on pages 134-5. Answer the following questions.
a) Select three aspects of Essex's personality or character that are evident in the portrait. Explain each of your selections. (6 marks)
b) What does Cecil mean by i) 'wit' and ii) 'delinquent'? (4 marks)
c) Cecil lists seven skills or qualities. Which does he value most highly? Explain your answer. (3 marks)
d) What reason does the extract give for thinking that Cecil was following in his family's tradition? (2 marks)

Preparing to answer questions on the political history of the reign of Elizabeth I as a whole

When you have completed your study of the period 1558-1603 - if you are using *Access to History* books, this will mean when you have also read John Warren's volume - you will need to pull all your work together. This will be a relatively demanding and time-consuming task but it is one that you will avoid at your peril. Only those who are extremely quick at thinking on their feet will be able to do this against the clock in the examination room. Most of those who have tried doing it in the past have come badly unstuck.

By the time you read these words you should have prepared notes on between eight and ten distinct topics on the political (domestic and foreign) and religious history of Elizabethan England. You should also be a long way towards reaching conclusions about the personality and character and the performance as queen of Elizabeth I. This will particularly be the case if you have followed the advice given at the end of chapter 1. If you have not yet done this, it would be a good idea to do so before proceeding further.

Now is the time to complete the drawing together of your ideas about Elizabeth herself. Presumably this will just be a matter of fitting the evidence you have gathered from outside this book - mainly on foreign affairs and religion - into the framework you have already developed. When you have done this you should find that you have several pieces of evidence to support each of the generalisations in your interpretation. This means that you will have far more material at your disposal than you could possibly use in one examination essay. This is the strongest possible argument in support of the necessity of thinking carefully about exactly what a particular examination question requires of you. How else are you to make sensible decisions about what to include and what to leave out? It also means that you are going to need to be experienced at including a generalisation and its supporting evidence in a single sentence. How else are you to cover the required amount of ground in an answer to a very general question? One useful way of preparing yourself to do this is to construct a set of revision notes on Elizabeth I made up of a number of sentences in a standard form such as 'Elizabeth was (generalisation) as she showed (the two or three most appropriate examples of this behaviour)'.

To focus on the person and performance of Elizabeth I is the most effective single way of developing a coherent picture of her reign, but it is unlikely to be sufficient on its own. Most students will feel a need to establish a chronological framework in their minds. If you have read pages 45-7 of this book you should already have a four-period model within which to organise the domestic political events of the reign. Now is the time to decide whether this model is of any help when considering foreign affairs and religion. Should it be a matter of concern if you find that a different set of periods is more helpful in making sense of these topics? What does this suggest about the status of such periods?

Historians have been interested in over-arching topics other than that of Elizabeth herself. The most frequently encountered involves the concept of 'threat' - threat to the régime and threat to the country. This has come about because one common way of perceiving the reign as a whole has been to see it as being made up of a short initial period during which the régime was established (the political and religious settlements), and a 40-year main period during which it was almost constantly under internal or external threat. In such accounts the historian's main tasks have been thought to be chronicling the threats and explaining why they were survived. This approach provides an interesting alternative structure for students to use when pulling the period together. Lists can be made of the threats. These can be organised chronologically or by type (for example, internal and external, or political and religious - how do you deal with those that overlap?). In each case the nature and the extent of the threat can be indicated and the reasons why it was survived can be explained. Other interesting questions are likely to spring to mind in the process. For example, what was the effect on the population as a whole of the long-term threat from abroad? Did this have anything to do with the British tradition of treating the régime and the country as being virtually synonymous?

Chronological Table

1533   7 September Elizabeth born

1558   17 November Elizabeth ascended the throne - Sir William Cecil appointed Permanent Secretary, Lord Robert Dudley appointed Master of the Horse

1559   first parliamentary session - religious settlement agreed

1562   Dudley and the Duke of Norfolk appointed to Privy Council

1563   second parliamentary session - agitation over marriage and the succession

1564   Dudley created Earl of Leicester

1565   Earl of Sussex appointed to Privy Council

1566   third parliamentary session - further agitation over marriage and the succession

1568   Mary, Queen of Scots, fled to England

1569   Revolt of the Northern Earls

1571   fourth parliamentary session - Cecil created Lord Burghley

1572   fifth parliamentary session - agitation over Mary, Queen of Scots, and the Duke of Norfolk executed
Burghley ceased to be Principal Secretary and became Lord Treasurer

1573   Sir Francis Walsingham appointed Secretary

1576   sixth parliamentary session

1579   Alençon match seemed likely

1581   seventh parliamentary session

1584   eighth parliamentary session

1586   ninth parliamentary session

1587   Mary, Queen of Scots, executed

1588   Spanish Armada, Leicester died

1589   tenth parliamentary session

1590   Walsingham died

1591   Sir Christopher Hatton died, Sir Robert Cecil appointed to Privy Council

1593   eleventh parliamentary session - Essex appointed to Privy Council

1597   twelfth parliamentary session - discontent over monopolies quietened by Elizabeth's promise to take action, Sir Robert Cecil appointed Principal Secretary

1598   Burghley died

1599   Essex's Irish expedition

1601   8 February Essex's attempted coup, 25 February Essex executed
thirteenth parliamentary session - Elizabeth's 'Golden Speech'

1603   24 March Elizabeth died

Further Reading

Considering the huge number of books that have been published on the period there are surprisingly few volumes that can be strongly recommended to the student wishing to delve more deeply into the political history of Elizabethan England.

Of the hundred or so different biographies of Elizabeth or histories of her reign that are to be found within the public library system, three stand out as being both accessible and particularly worthy of being read from cover to cover.

J.E. Neale's *Queen Elizabeth I,* although published as long ago as the 1930s, remains one of the outstanding brief political biographies in the English language. It is essential reading for all those who wish to acquire a 'feel' for the way in which Elizabethan political history used to be perceived. Quite naturally the student needs to keep his or her critical faculties alert at all times when reading it as the picture that Neale presents is clearly more favourable than would currently be thought warranted, but many of the insights provided remain very perceptive.

Christopher Haigh's *Elizabeth I* (Longman 1988) brings together the findings of the first flush of revisionist writings. Haigh is by far the most lucid and thought provoking of those who have challenged the old orthodoxy established by J.E. Neale and Conyers Read.

Wallace McCaffrey's *Elizabeth I* (Edward Arnold 1993) is an academic work of very high quaiity. Its American author has synthesised his own lifetime's work on the period and the recently published findings of others to produce a book that would make a very valuable core text for those studying Elizabeth's reign in detail.

There are, of course, many books that would repay being dipped into in order to gain a flavour of the way in which their authors have approached their task. Any of the writings of **Conyers Read** would be worth sampling, although in terms of availability and of relevance to this book his two volumes on Sir William Cecil *(Mr Secretary Cecil and Queen Elizabeth* (1955), and *Lord Burghley and Queen Elizabeth* (1960)) would be most appropriate. A feel for the debate over Elizabeth and Parliament could quite speedily be acquired by looking at **J.E. Neale,** *Elizabeth I and her Parliaments* (2 vols, 1953 and 1957) and **G.R. Elton,** *The Parliament of England, 1559-81* (Cambridge 1986).

Readers who wish to track down works on particular aspects of the period would do well to start with the extensive bibliography in **John Guy,** *Tudor England* (OUP 1988).

Index

When searchings for a particular piece of information it may be helpful to use the Contents and Chronological Table as well as this Index.

142   Index